Biblical Worldview II
Applying a Biblical Worldview
BWVW 102

Steve Putney
Liberty University

Biblical Worldview II: Applying a Biblical Worldview – BWVW 102
Copyright © 2012 by Stephen Putney, DMin

Scripture taken from the Holy Bible, King James Version, New Living Translation, New International Version, English Standard Version and New English Translation.

Permissions Department
Academx Publishing Services, Inc.
P.O. Box 56527
Virginia Beach, VA 23456

Printed in the United States of America

ISBN-10: 1-60036-554-X
ISBN-13: 978-1-60036-554-6

CONTENTS

WORLDVIEW REVIEW

What Does The Bible Say About Worldview?

1. **Genesis 1:1 (KJV)** - In the beginning God created the heaven and the earth.

2. **Job 14:14 (NIV)** - If a man dies, will he live again? All the days of my hard service I will wait for my renewal to come.

3. **Romans 12:1-2 (NIV)** - Therefore, I urge you, brothers, in view of God's mercy, to offer your bodies as living sacrifices, holy and pleasing to God—this is your spiritual act of worship. Do not conform any longer to the pattern of this world, but be transformed by the renewing of your mind. Then you will be able to test and approve what God's will is—his good, pleasing and perfect will.

4. **Acts 28 1-6** - Notice the reaction of the people based upon their worldview.

What is a worldview?

Do I have a worldview?

I. WHAT A WORLDVIEW IS NOT

A. It is _____ merely our _____ of the world. "Our society is really sinful."

B. It is not limited to those who study _____.

II. WHAT IS A WORLDVIEW?

A. It is your _____ of life.

B. It is the basis for your _____ decision making.

C. It is a map of reality that provides answers to the ultimate questions of life.

D. Simply put: A "Worldview" is: <u>the way you view the world and make value judgments about life.</u>

E. It's like looking through colored glasses that affect _____ we see.

F. Quotes about worldview:

    a. "A worldview, whether Christian or secular, is the unifying perspective from which we organize our thinking about life, death, art, science, faith, learning, work, money, values, and morals. A worldview is our underlying philosophy of life" - Ken Hemphill, *Life Answers*, (Lifeway Press, 1993).

    b. The "overarching framework to bring unity to our lives." – Pearcey, p. 17. "God's Word becomes a set of glasses offering a new perspective on all our thoughts and actions." – p. 24

    c. "An ordered set of propositions that one believes especially propositions about life's most important questions." – Moreland, p. 13 – Phil. Found.

    d. We need to draw from all areas of knowledge in forming an integrated Christian worldview consistent with Scripture – p. 17

    e. A view of the world and human kinds place in it. Colson

    f. Your worldview is the way you believe the world works and how you fit into it. Colson p. 57

    g. A worldview is a commitment, a fundamental orientation of the heart, that can be expressed as a story or in a set of presuppositions (assumptions which may be true, partially true, or entirely false) which we hold (consciously or subconsciously, consistently or inconsistently) about the basic constitution of reality, and that provides the foundation on which we live and move have our being. – James Sire, Naming the Elephant, 122.

G. Many people do not think seriously about their worldview until a <u>crisis</u> causes them to question life.

H. It (Worldview) answers questions like:

    1) The question of _____.

- How did life begin in the first place?

- Where did I come from?

- Genesis 1:1, 26-27

    2) The question of _____.

- What does it mean to be a human?

- Am I more important than animals?

- Genesis 1:27-28; Romans 3:23

3) The question of _____ (purpose).

- Why are we here?

- Why am I here?

- Matthew 22:37-40; Matthew 28:18-20

4) The question of _____ (ethics).

- What is meant by right and wrong?

- How should I live?

- Matthew 22:37-40

5) The question of _____.

- Is there life after death?

- What will happen to me when I die?

- Will I have to answer for the choices I made and how I lived my life?

- Hebrews 9:27-28; Philippians 1:21, 23; Revelation 20:11-15

I. Look through your biblical worldview and see the value of human life. Your worldview affects your view of abortion, euthanasia, sexual relationships, marriage, gender issues, poverty, work, racial issues, etc.

III. THE BASIS OF A CHRISTIAN WORLDVIEW

A. _____ _____ - (Genesis 1:1).

B. God has _____ Himself to mankind - (Hebrews 1:1-2).

C. Man's greatest problem is _____ – (Romans 3:23, 6:23).

D. _____ _____ is God's son who is the redeemer of the world - (John 3:16).

E. The Bible is God's _____ - (2 Timothy 3:16; 2 Peter 1:20-21).

F. Christians are to follow the teachings of the _____ - (2 Timothy 3:16-17; 1 Peter 1:16).

> "A biblical worldview is foundational for accurately interpreting reality in a manner that coincides with God's revealed truths."
> – Robert Velarde, *What Einstein's Brain Can Teach Us About Worldviews*,

Why is your worldview so important?

> • "A worldview is the filter we use, consciously or subconsciously, to interpret our world and what happens in it." – Robert Velarde, *What Einstein's Brain Can Teach Us About*

It is a way of looking at the world based on the Word of God.

Our worldview must have a firm _____ if we will establish consistent _____ standards.

What areas of life are affected by your worldview?

Name one current news item, recent movie, or personal decision you have made that has been affected significantly by your worldview:

CHRISTIAN/COMMUNITY SERVICE (CSER)

The following information needs to be read and understood by *both Liberty students and supervisors who work with Liberty students*. Any questions or concerns not covered by the following policies should be directed to the CSER office.

Location – Green Hall (GH) 1880
Hours – M-F 8:00 a.m. – 4:30 p.m.
Phone – (434) 582-2325
Fax – (434) 582-2660
Email – cser@liberty.edu

To fulfill Christian/Community Service (CSER) graduation requirements, students and supervisors must understand particular aspects about four areas: **I) Criteria, II) Enrollment, III) Participation**, and **IV) Evaluation & Credit**. The following policies are arranged in an FAQ format to facilitate understanding.

Section 1 - Criteria

A. What qualifies as a valid CSER?
  1. To receive CSER credit students may not:
   a. Receive monetary compensation
   b. Receive academic credit
   c. Be awarded a scholarship

  2. A CSER must fit within the framework of the <u>missions and goals</u> **of the department, which may include any, or all, of the following:**
   a. Evangelism
   b. Discipleship
   c. Tutoring/mentoring
   d. Civic and community services (this does not include political campaigning)
   e. Community improvement
   f. Alleviation of human suffering
   g. Assisting the underprivileged and less fortunate
   h. Education and development of children/adults
   i. Educational assistance

j. Stewardship of the earth (Environmental projects, care for animals, etc.)

See our listing of CSER opportunities that fit these criteria.

B. Can a CSER be fulfilled with an organization other than is listed?

Yes. This falls under the areas of Special Projects (399s) and Church Extensions (279s) and requires special application. In these cases, there must be strict adherence to the following:

1. Special Projects (399s)
a. Students are expected to respect the doctrinal and ethical positions of Liberty University.
b. Students must make application and receive approval through the Center for CSER prior to receiving credit.

2. Church Extensions (279s)
a. Students are expected to respect the doctrinal and ethical positions of Liberty University.
b. Students must make application and receive approval through the Center for CSER prior to receiving credit.
c. The Center for CSER requires a doctrinal statement from a prospective church. The church will be evaluated in light of the University's doctrinal statement.

Note: *Without prior approval from the Center for CSER for 279s and 399s, students run the risk of having their CSERs denied due to their failure to conform to established CSER criteria.*

C. Can a CSER be done with a for-profit business or organization?

While the general rule is that CSERs must be done through existing non-profit 501(c)(3) organizations, it is possible that some for-profit organizations, particularly those dealing with human health and services (hospitals, nursing homes, etc.), may be approved as CSER sites. Further, if a business is involved in a not-for-profit community service endeavor, this *may* be considered a valid CSER opportunity provided the minimal 20 hours (See Section III.C.) can be completed. *Strict guidelines must be followed in these situations. Requests for exceptions will be dealt with on a case by case basis. It is mandatory that students make application and receive approval through the Center for CSER prior to receiving credit.*

Note: Without prior approval from the Center for CSER, students run the risk of having their CSERs denied due to their failure to conform to established CSER criteria.

D. May students use their internship at a non-profit organization for a CSER?
While you may not receive CSER credit for the work for which you are being paid or are receiving academic credit (Section I.A.1), you may do additional hours for CSER credit. Each situation will be handled on a case by case basis.

Note: Internships at for-profit organizations may not be used for CSER credit.

E. Can students fulfill their CSERs by volunteering at someone's home?
No. Any exceptions to this policy require CSER approval.

Note: Without prior approval from the Center for CSER, students run the risk of having their CSERs denied due to their failure to conform to established CSER criteria.

Section II: Enrollment

A. Who must enroll in CSER?
1. All residential undergraduate students who are full-time during the fall or spring semester are required to be enrolled in a CSER. Undergraduate students are considered full-time if they are taking twelve (12) or more credit hours in a given semester.

2. According to the student's Degree Completion Plan (DCP), BWVW 101 and BWVW 102 are a student's first two CSER requirements.

B. What are BWVW 101 and BWVW 102?
According to the student's Degree Completion Plan (DCP), BWVW 101 and BWVW 102 are a student's first two CSER requirements.

1. **BWVW 101: BIBLICAL WORLDVIEW I**
This course is designed to aid the student in the development of a biblical worldview. This will involve an introduction to critical thinking, an evaluation of contemporary moral philosophies, and an affirmation of absolute truth. Students will be challenged to integrate a biblical worldview into their Christian/Community Service.
BWVW 101 is a Prerequisite for BWVW 102

2. **BWVW 102: BIBLICAL WORLDVIEW II**
This course is a study of contemporary moral issues encountered by students in their Christian/Community Service. Students will be challenged to evaluate these issues and understand their responsibilities to them in light of a biblical worldview.
Prerequisite: BWVW 101

Note: Students who have failed either or both BWVWs will be required to enroll in the needed CSERs to keep from falling behind in their graduation requirements. These students will be doing CSER while simultaneously completing their BWVW requirements.

C. When may a student enroll in a CSER?
Students may enroll during the fall, spring or summer semesters.

Note: Although CSER is not required during the summer semester, a CSER earned over the summer may count for a previous or future semester (See details at Section IV.G.)

1. **FALL SEMESTER** - The Christian/Community Service Registration Fair occurs during the first week of the fall semester. CSER supervisors are invited to represent their area of service and register students. Students are not required to register during the fair, but are encouraged to do so. Otherwise, they are responsible to register through the Center for CSER before the Add/Drop deadline.
The Add/Drop deadline for the FALL semester is the first Monday in October. A $10.00 late fee will be added to the student's Liberty University account after this date.

Note: CSERs REGISTERED FOR IN THE FALL WILL AUTOMATICALLY CARRY OVER TO THE SPRING SEMESTER, BUT NOT THE SUMMER SEMESTER. *Students must understand that they are making a* **one-year commitment** *to the organization when they enroll in the fall semester.* If they wish to change CSERs in the spring, they must follow the proper procedures (See Section II.E. below).

2. **SPRING SEMESTER** – There is no Registration Fair in the spring semester. Consequently, students enrolling in CSER for the spring semester are responsible to register through the Center for CSER by the Add/Drop deadline.
The Add/Drop deadline for the SPRING semester is the first Monday in March. A $10.00 late fee will be added to the student's Liberty University account after this date.

3. **SUMMER SEMESTER** - Students must complete the appropriate forms and obtain the necessary signatures before they can receive credit for a summer CSER. Students must obtain these forms in the Center for CSER. If possible, it is recommended that students finalize their summer CSER enrollments prior to leaving at the end of the spring semester. Otherwise, they are responsible to register through the Center for CSER before the Add/Drop deadline.

The Add/Drop deadline for the SUMMER semester is the first Monday in July. A $10.00 late fee will be added to the student's Liberty University account after this date.

Note: Winter Break is not an official CSER semester, but students may use the break between the fall and spring semesters to make up missed CSERs should they fall behind (See Section III.F.). If a student wishes to use the break for this purpose, they must make application and receive approval through the Center for CSER prior to receiving credit. Without prior approval from the Center for CSER, students run the risk of having their CSERs denied due to their failure to conform to established CSER criteria.
All hours must be completed within the Winter Break.

Special note on Winterfest: *Effective fall 2009 Winterfest will no longer be applied to a student's spring semester of the following year. This CSER opportunity may be used for students' fall semester CSERs of the same year or, like any other CSER, to catch up if they fall behind in previous semesters.*

D. Do students need to re-register their fall CSERs in the spring semester?
No. CSERs REGISTERED FOR IN THE FALL WILL AUTOMATICALLY CARRY OVER TO THE SPRING SEMESTER, BUT NOT THE SUMMER SEMESTER. *Students must understand that they are making a **one-year commitment** to the organization when they enroll in the fall semester.*

E. May students change (Add/Drop) their CSERs?
Yes. Students wishing to change a CSER for which they are registered must obtain signed permission from their CSER supervisor and receive approval from the Center for CSER. The appropriate CSER Add/Drop form is available in the Center for CSER.

Note: *A $10.00 late fee will be applied to every drop and every add after the deadline of a given semester. (See Add/Drop Deadlines in Section II.C.1-3 above.).*

Section III: Participation

A. How many CSERs must students complete?
To graduate from Liberty, all full-time, residential undergraduate students must successfully complete one CSER requirement for each full-time semester that they are a student, up to eight (8) semesters. Undergraduate students must pass BWVW 101 and 102 which are their first two (2) semesters of CSER requirements (See II.B.). They must then successfully complete at least one CSER for each full-time semester that they are enrolled, up to six (6) more

semesters. Once students have fulfilled these requirements, they will no longer need to enroll in a CSER.

Note: Residential students who are full-time (12 hours or more) are required to enroll in CSER whether they are taking residential or LU Online courses.

B. How many CSERs may students do during a semester?

While students are only *required* to complete one CSER for every semester they are full-time, they may register and receive a grade for more than one CSER during any semester (Refer to Section IV.F. for restrictions concerning credit for future semesters). Students who fall behind and need to receive credit for more than one CSER in a semester to fulfill their graduation requirements, must get permission from the Center for CSER to do a double CSER. (See Section III.F. below).

C. How much time will a CSER require?

Students must complete a *minimum* of 20 hours in order to pass any CSER. Some supervisors may require more than 20 hours. In such cases, supervisors will inform students prior to enrollment, and then the student must complete the additional hours to pass his or her CSER with that organization. (Examples: Young Life and the local hospitals; LGH and VBH).

D. May students complete their CSER requirement during multiple semesters?

No. Students must complete all CSER hours for a registered CSER within that semester only. Semester beginning and ending dates are according to the official calendar issued be the Registrar's office. Summer semester and Winter Break hours must be *completed* between the spring and fall and fall and spring semesters respectively.

E. May students complete their CSER requirement through multiple organizations or supervisors?

No. In order to receive credit toward the fulfillment of each CSER requirement students will complete their registered CSER with one organization only and every registered CSER must be completed under one CSER supervisor only.

F. What if students fall behind in CSER?

Students may make up their CSER requirements in later semesters by completing more than one CSER in a semester. They may use the winter break to catch up as well (See Note in Section II.C. above). Students may only complete a maximum of two (2) CSERS with one CSER registration. IT IS MANDATORY THAT STUDENTS APPLY FOR APPROVAL THROUGH THE CENTER FOR CSER BEFORE CREDIT WILL BE GIVEN FOR ANY MORE THAN ONE CSER PER SEMESTER.

G. What if a student receives an "F" for CSER?

The grade of "F" will remain on the student's transcript for that CSER and will not count toward fulfilling the graduation requirement unless the grade is changed through one of three ways:

1. **The Repeat Policy:** Students wishing to change a failing grade must repeat and pass *that same CSER* under the CSER repeat policy. It is mandatory that students apply for the repeat policy through the Center for CSER before credit will be given.

2. **Add/Drop:** Students may need to see their supervisor to process a Add/Drop form. Supervisors have full authority to deny dropping the students' CSER and in that case the Center for CSER may not change the "F." The student may then use the Repeat Policy.

3. **Missing Service Evaluation Form:** Students may simply have failed to turn in their completed Service Evaluation form, and doing so will correct this situation (See Section IV.A. for details).

Section IV: Evaluation and Credit

A. What is the CSER evaluation process?

This process is central to the CSER program. Upon registration for a CSER, students will need a Liberty University Christian/Community Service Evaluation form (the "blue" form). When the student fulfills their hours for a registered CSER, this form must be completed before the Center for CSER will accept it. Students are responsible to make sure that their *exact dates and hours* have been logged, that they have done the student reflection and that they have met with their supervisor to receive their final evaluation, grade and supervisor's signature. IT IS THE STUDENT'S RESPONSIBILITY TO RETURN THE COMPLETED FORM TO THE CENTER FOR CSER BY THE POSTED DEADLINE. (This deadline date is posted on the CSER calendar and will be announced via a university-wide e-mail and a Splash page notification within a week of the time it is due at the end of the semester).

B. How will students be graded for their CSER?

Each student will receive a letter grade of A, B, C, D or F, according to the following criteria:

A - student displays exceptional service; excellent attitude; volunteered at least 20 hours

B - displays satisfactory service; punctuality; appropriate attitude; volunteered at least 20 hours

C - displays acceptable service; usually punctual; acceptable attitude;

volunteered at least 20 hours

D - displays unsatisfactory service; not punctual; volunteered at least 20 hours

F - designates "failure"; unacceptable service; volunteered less than 20 hours

Note: Supervisors will also be required to validate each student's hours, and write out a brief personal evaluation of each student. No incomplete evaluation sheet will be accepted, and no evaluation form will be accepted without the supervisor's signature. It is the STUDENT'S responsibility to return the final evaluation and grade form to the Center for CSER by the posted deadline. (This deadline date is posted on the CSER calendar and will be announced on the Splash page within a week of the time it is due at the end of the semester).

C. How may students inquire about their CSER status?

Students who have questions or concerns regarding their CSER history and status should direct them to the Center for CSER.

Location and Hours: Green Hall 1880
M-F 8:00 a.m. - 4:30 p. m.
Phone: (434) 582-2325
E-mail: cser@liberty.edu

D. What should students do if there is a question or conflict concerning their registered CSER?

All questions regarding schedules, accountability procedures, grades or conflicts of any nature concerning a student's specific CSER should be initially directed to the student's supervisor for that CSER. If a satisfactory solution does not result from this meeting, the student should then contact the Center for CSER for further assistance.

E. May students receive credit for a CSER done in a previous semester for which they did not register?

Yes. However, it must meet all previously established criteria (See Section I.A.). Further, the student must complete the appropriate paperwork and receive permission from the Center for CSER. By not getting prior approval the student runs the risk of having their request for credit denied due to their not meeting the established criteria.
A $10.00 late registration fee will be added to the student's Liberty University account for each CSER.

F. May students complete extra CSERs in the fall or spring semester to count for a future semester?

No. The only semester in which a CSER may be applied to a future semester is the summer semester; otherwise, students cannot get ahead in their CSERs. (See next question for how summer credits will be applied). Additional CSERs done while the student is taking BWVW (except for summer CSERs) will not count toward future requirements either, unless the student has failed either or both BWVWs (See Section II.B. above).

G. How will CSERs completed during the summer semester be applied?

Summer CSERs may be used for a previous or future semester, however, only **one** CSER per summer semester may be applied toward a future semester.

H. How will grades received for CSER affect students' GPAs?

Grades received in BWVW 101 and BWVW 102 will become a permanent part of students GPAs. Grades received for CSER will not affect their GPA, however, they will be recorded as a standard letter grade and become a permanent part of the student's school transcript.

Faculty and Staff

Dr. Lew Weider, Professor, Director
Dr. Troy Matthews, Associate Professor, Associate Director
Dr. Steve Putney, Associate Professor, Assistant Director
Dr. Rob Van Engen, Assistant Professor, Assistant Director
Dr. Will Honeycutt, Assistant Professor, Assistant Director
Mr. Darren Wu, Assistant Professor, CSER Coordinator
Mrs. Jessica Rosewell, CSER Registrar
Bethany Burnette, Office Manager

ABORTION

Do you know someone who has had an abortion?

What is the stated issue behind the abortion controversy today (according to those who are pro-choice, pro-life)?

> Pro-choice -

> Pro-life -

What does the Bible say about Abortion?

Psalm 139:13, 15 (NKJV) - "For you formed my inward parts, you covered me **in my mother's womb**." "My frame was not hidden from you when I was made in secret, and skillfully wrought in the lowest parts of the earth."

Jeremiah 1:5 (NIV) - "Before I formed you in the womb I knew you, before you were born I set you apart; I appointed you as a prophet to the nations."

Genesis 1:27 (ESV) - So God created man in his own image, in the image of God he created him; male and female he created them.

I. An Overview of Abortion in the United States

Developed by Physicians for Reproductive Choice and Health® (PRCH) and The Alan Guttmacher Institute (AGI) (research arm of Planned Parenthood)

Unintended Pregnancies
(Approximately 3.0 Million Annually)

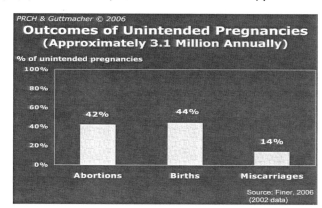

Important names to know:

PP – Planned Parenthood

AGI – Alan Guttmacher Institute

NARAL – National Abortion Rights Action League

NRLC – National Right to Life Committee

➢ In 2008, some 1.21 million pregnancies were terminated by abortion in the United States.

➢ Some ___% of all women aged 15–44 had an abortion in 2002.

➢ Abortion is one of the most common _____ procedures in the United States.

➢ By age 20, 1 in 7 women have had at least one abortion; by age 45, 4 in 10 have done so.

> **ABORTION**: the deliberate termination of a human being from the moment of conception until just prior to birth. This term is often made to sound innocuous. However, in an abortion, not only is the pregnancy or the product of conception terminated, so is a human life!

Does life have value, even if it not normal?

Annual Number of Abortions Per 1,000 Women Aged 15–44

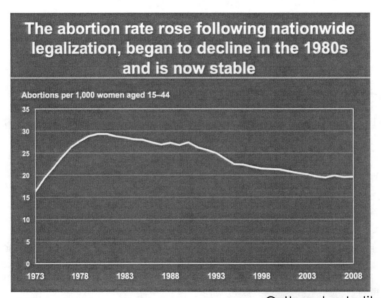

Guttmacher Institute, July 2008

Numbers and Rates:
Global and regional estimates of induced abortion,
1995, 2003 and 2008

Region	No. of abortions (millions)			Abortion rate*		
	1995	2003	2008	1995	2003	2008
World	45.6	41.6	43.8	35	29	28
Developed countries	10.0	6.6	6.0	39	25	24
Excluding Eastern Europe	3.8	3.5	3.2	20	19	17
Developing countries	35.5	35.0	37.8	34	29	29
Excluding China	24.9	26.4	28.6	33	30	29
Africa	5.0	5.6	6.4	33	29	29
Asia	26.8	25.9	27.3	33	29	28
Europe	7.7	4.3	4.2	48	28	27
Latin America	4.2	4.1	4.4	37	31	32
North America	1.5	1.5	1.4	22	21	19
Oceania	0.1	0.1	0.1	21	18	17

*Abortions per 1,000 women aged 15–44.
Source: Sedgh G et al., Induced abortion: incidence and trends worldwide from 1995 to 2008, *Lancet*, 2012 (forthcoming).

GUTTMACHER INSTITUTE

What is the main reason we are told that women have abortions?

Most Important Reason Given for Terminating an Unwanted Pregnancy

1. Inadequate _____ 21%

2. Not ready for _____ 21%

3. Woman's life would be changed too much 16%

4. Problems with relationship; _____ 12%

5. Too _____ - not mature enough 11%

6. Children are grown woman has all she wants 8%

7. Fetus has possible _____ problem 3%

8. Woman has health problem 1%

9. Pregnancy caused by _____ or _____ 1%

10. Other 4%

11. Average number of reasons given 3.7%

Source: Torres and Forrest, 1988

17

Most Important Reason Given for Terminating an Unwanted Pregnancy
AGI Survey 2004

1. Unready   25%
2. Can't _____ baby now   23%
3. Has all the children she wanted or all children are grown   19%
4. Problems with relationships or wants to avoid single parenthood 8%
5. Too _____ or young to have child   7%
6. Other   6%
7. Interfere with education or career plans   4%
8. Mother has _____ problems   4%
9. Possible fetal health problems   3%
10. Husband/partner wants her to have abortion   <0.5%
11. Woman's parents want her to have abortion   <0.5%
12. _____ or _____   <0.5%

AGI, 2004

For information about abortion from a pro-life perspective:
http://www.nrlc.org/abortion/index.html)

Commonly Used Terms:

✓ _____: reproductive cell (sperm/ovum)

✓ _____: formed by the union of male and female gametes (fertilization)

✓ _____: the unborn from fertilization up to 3 months

✓ _____: 3 months to birth.

II. Abortion: Legal History in the United States.

   A. Prior to Roe V. Wade, most states made abortion a crime except for saving the mother.

B. Legal cases that led to Roe V. Wade

   1. _____ v. _____ - Decided June 7, 1965

   "Right to privacy"

   2. _____ v. _____ - Decided March 22, 1972

   "Right to privacy"

C. _____ v _____ - Jan. 22, 1973

   Main Ruling - Lifted bans on abortion in all 50 states A woman's "right to privacy" extends to her liberty to terminate an unwanted pregnancy.
   Also: The unborn are not "persons" and thus ineligible for constitutional protection.

   Key person: Jane Roe (Norma McCorvey) -

   What the Supreme Court declared:

   - "The Constitution does not define 'person'..."

   - "person" has "application only postnatally"

   - "The word 'person' as used in the Fourteenth Amendment, does not include the unborn."

**The unborn are essentially non-persons
and do not fall under the protection of the 4th or 14th Amendments.**

IV Amendment to the U.S. Constitution - "The right of the people to be secure in their persons, houses, papers, and effects, against unreasonable searches and seizures, shall not be violated, ..."

Amendment XIV Section 1 to the U.S. Constitution - All persons born or naturalized in the United States, and subject to the jurisdiction thereof, are citizens of the United States... nor shall any State deprive any person of life, liberty, or property, without due process of law; nor deny to any person within its jurisdiction the equal protection of the laws.

D. Other Important Cases

    1. _____ v _____ - Jan. 22, 1973

Main ruling - Expanded definition of "health" of the mother to include familial, financial, psychological, well-being, etc. as determined by her physician.

    2. _____ _____ v _____ - 1992

Main ruling - Discarded 3 trimester of Roe and focused on the "viability" of the fetus as the determining point where a state's interest in unborn life begins.

    3. Partial-Birth Abortion Ban Act – 2003

WASHINGTON, D.C. -- President Bush signed the Partial-Birth Abortion Ban Act (S. 3) into law on November 5, 2003, The bill represents the first direct national restriction on any method of abortion since the Supreme Court legalized abortion on demand in 1973.

III. Types of Abortion

    A. _____ & Aspiration

- Used on 80% of abortions up to 12th week of pregnancy
- Mouth of the cervix is dilated
- Hollow tube with knifelike edged tip is inserted into the womb
- A suction machine with force 28 times greater than a vacuum cleaner literally rips the developing baby to pieces and sucks the remains into a container to be disposed

    B. Dilation and Curettage

- Dilate cervix to allow the insertion of curetta—a loop-shaped knife—into the womb
- Instrument scrapes placenta from the uterus and cuts baby apart; pieces are drawn through the cervix
- Baby is _____ to be sure that all parts are accounted for
- If parts are left inside, the mother could bleed or become infected

C. RU 486

- Synthetic steroid used 5-7 weeks after conception
- Deprives baby of vital nutritional hormone progesterone
- Child _____ to death as nutrient lining of the womb sloughs off
- Delivery of a dead baby

D. Dilation and Evacuation

- Used between 12 and 24 weeks
- The child is cut to pieces by a sharp knife, as in D & C
- The child is much larger and far more developed
- The child weighs as much as a <u>pound</u> and is as much as a <u>foot</u> in length

E. _____ Injection

- Amniotic fluid is removed and replaced with a toxic saline solution
- Baby ingest the toxins and dies 1-2 hours later from salt poisoning, dehydration, and hemorrhaging
- 24 hours later the mother goes into labor delivering a dead baby
- Chemical burning of the skin causes a painful death for the baby

F. Prostaglandin

- Prostaglandin hormones are injected into womb or released in
- Vaginal suppository cause uterus to contract and deliver baby _____
- Sometimes a saline solution is used to kill baby before the premature birth

G. Partial-birth abortion

- Guided by ultrasound, the abortionist grabs the baby's legs with forceps
- The baby's leg is pulled out into the birth canal
- The abortionist delivers the baby's entire body, except for the _____
- The abortionist jams _____ into the baby's skull. The scissors are then opened to enlarge the skull
- The scissors are removed and a suction catheter is inserted. The child's _____ are sucked out, causing the skull to collapse. The dead baby is then removed

H. Hysterotomy

- Used in <u>last</u> trimester
- Baby removed as in a Cesarean birth
- Baby set aside and allowed to die or killed by a deliberate act

I. Morning after pill

- High-powered birth control pill

Search for articles by Randy Alcorn, John Piper, John Stott, John Ankerberg, Kerby Anderson

J. Birth control pill

- Prevent ovulation
- Stop conception by thickening cervical mucus
- Stop implantation – by thinning the uterine wall

How about selective reduction? What does my worldview tell me?

IV. The Key Question: When does life begin?

- _____
- _____
- Brainwave activity
- _____
- Partial Birth
- _____
- Personality Development

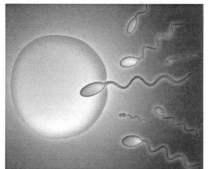

V. Arguments Supporting That a New Life Begins at Conception

A. Arguments from _____

> "Many people mistakenly feel that abortion is a "religious" issue. But it is not. It is a scientific issue, and specifically, a biological issue." - http://www.johnankerberg.org/Articles/apologetics/AP0805W3.htm

> **Dr. Keith L. Moore, Professor and Chairman of the Department of Anatomy, University of Toronto** - Essentials of Human Embryology states: "Human development is a continuous process that begins when an ovum from a female is fertilized by a sperm from a male. Growth and differentiation transform the zygote, a single cell… into a multicellar adult human being." It is also written, "…human

22

development begins at fertilization..." - embryologists Keith Moore and T.V. N. Persaud in *The Developing Human* (7th edition, 2003), the most widely used textbook on human embryology.

➢ **Professor** Micheline **Matthews-Roth, Harvard University Medical School:** She testified before a Senate Judiciary Subcommittee on April 26, 1981, "It is scientifically correct to say that an individual human life begins at conception, when egg and sperm join to form the zygote, and that this developing human always is a member of our species in all stages of life." - http://topics.nytimes.com/top/reference/timestopics/subjects/a/abortion/index. html?s=oldest&offset=70&inline=nyt-classifier

B. Arguments from the _____

- The unborn are known by _____.

    Before I formed you in the womb I knew you, before you were born I set you apart; I appointed you as a prophet to the nations – Jeremiah 1:5. *You made all the delicate, inner parts of my body and knit me together in my mother's womb* – Psalm 139:13. Also see Job 31:15.

- The life of the unborn is protected by the same punishment for injury or death as that of an _____.

    Now suppose two men are fighting, and in the process they accidentally strike a pregnant woman so she gives birth prematurely. If no further injury results, the man who struck the woman must pay the amount of compensation the woman's husband demands and the judges approve. But if there is further injury, the punishment must match the injury: a life for a life – Exodus 21:22-23.

- The unborn are called by God before _____.
    Listen to me, all you in distant lands! Pay attention, you who are far away! The LORD called me before my birth; from within the womb he called me by name – Isaiah 49:1. See also Genesis 25:22-23; Judges 13:2-7.

- _____ babies are called "children".
    At the sound of Mary's greeting, Elizabeth's child leaped within her, and Elizabeth was filled with the Holy Spirit. When I heard your greeting, the baby in my womb jumped for joy – Luke 1:41, 44. See also Exodus 21:22.

- The same Greek word (brephos) is used for a baby inside the womb and outside the womb.
    And you will recognize him by this sign: You will find a baby wrapped snugly in strips of cloth, lying in a manger – Luke 2:12.
    See also Luke 1:41, 44; 2:16; 18:15; Acts 7:19; 2 Timothy 3:15.

- Christ was human from the point of _____.
    See Matthew 1:18, Luke 1:35.

- Unborn children possess _____ characteristics such as sin.
    For I was born a sinner—yes, from the moment my mother conceived me – Psalm 51:5.
    They also experience joy. See Luke 1:41, 44.
    These characteristics are distinctive of persons.

VI. Arguing Abortion: (Pro & Con)

*"Now how should [the question of the personhood of the fetus] be decided? Is it a **legal** question, a **constitutional** question, a **medical** question, a **philosophical** question, a **religious** question, or what is it?*
- Justice Harry Blackmun (Chief Justice and author of opinion of the court for Roe v. Wade)

What are the main arguments *for* abortion?

1. Nearly all abortions take place in the first trimester, when a fetus cannot exist independent of the mother.
2. The concept of personhood is different from the concept of human life.
3. Adoption is not an alternative to abortion, because it remains the woman's choice whether or not to give her child up for adoption.
4. Abortion is a safe medical procedure.
5. In the case of rape or incest, forcing a woman made pregnant by this violent act would cause further psychological harm to the victim.
6. Abortion is not used as a form of contraception.
7. The ability of a woman to have control of her body is critical to civil rights.
8. Taxpayer dollars are used to enable poor women to access the same medical services as rich women, and abortion is one of these services.
9. Teenagers who become mothers have grim prospects for the future.
10. Like any other difficult situation, abortion creates stress. Yet the American Psychological Association found that stress was greatest prior to an abortion, and that there was no evidence of post-abortion syndrome.
    http://womensissues.about.com/od/reproductiverights/a/AbortionArgumen.htm

Use your critical thinking skills to examine these arguments.

Four main areas for arguing the abortion question (against):

1. _____

> **Focus:** To argue that in the event we are not sure that human life exists, legally, we should err on the side of protecting life, rather than taking it or even acting in way that may potentially result in its death.
>
> **Rationale:** All persons in the US have a constitutionally protected "right to life." The Supreme Court could not determine when personhood begins. From a legal standpoint, it is better to err on the side of life in order to protect it.
> The burden of proof should be with the life-taker, and the benefit of the doubt with the lifesaver.
>
> **Responding to pro-choice claims:**
> *"Women have a legal right to control their bodies in whatever way they want."*
>
> **First** - No one has an unconditional (unqualified) legal right to do with their body whatever they wish, especially if it threatens to harm or kill another person.
> **Second** - In pregnancy there are two distinct bodies (i.e. individuals) involved, not just one.
>
> *"Well, I am against abortion, personally, but we should not seek to legally impose our personal morality on those who think otherwise."*
>
> **First -** When it comes to the life and death of human beings, laws are constantly imposed on us regardless of our beliefs to the contrary. Laws do not prevent the activity from happening, but they no doubt curtail it.
> **Second -** Argument from analogy – "I don't believe in slavery, personally, and will never own a slave, but I would not want to legally impose my views about slavery on someone who does believe in it."

2. _____

> **Focus:** To argue that if personhood does not begin at the moment of conception/fertilization, then our value as humans is not <u>intrinsic</u>. How much is a human life worth, and when does it have such worth? If not from conception, then human worth becomes dependent upon some other humans' arbitrary, conflicting and changing definitions of personhood.
>
> **Rationale:** Once human life has been devalued at one stage of development, then it is easy to devalue it at successive stages of development, and it becomes difficult to protect human life if

someone in authority (with legal and political power) considers a life "not worth living." Remember: The defense of the unborn is, ultimately, the defense of the human race.

3. _____

> **Focus**: To counter the pro-choice idea that the unborn are nothing more than another "part" of the mother's body, and thus she should be able to do anything with *her* body that she chooses. Emphasize the individuality of our prenatal existence.

> **Rationale**: A consideration of every "milestone" of fetal development from conception to the status of so-called "viability," the point, at which humans are said, under current abortion law, to have a right to life, will clearly show our *individuality*. We are *never* merely a part of our mother's body, but a unique individual from the time of conception to the moment of live birth.

4. _____

> **Focus:** To show two things.
> 1) While the Bible does not explicitly state that the unborn are persons, or "created in the image of God" it consistently uses language that takes this notion for granted, making it unnecessary to argue the point.
> 2) While the Bible does not explicitly forbid "abortion," it does forbid murder on account of humans being created "in the image of God," and, as stated above, the unborn (including Jesus when He was a zygote, embryo, and fetus prior to birth) are assumed to be in the image of God (in Christ's case God incarnate).

> (See prior notes: arguments From Scripture)

VI. A HELPING STRATEGY: *The Woman Considering an Abortion*

1) Commend her for calling.

2) Tactfully remind her that she quite possibly has strong feelings about the moral implications of abortion or she wouldn't have called.

> *Taken from: The Billy Graham Workers Handbook (found online)*

3) Avoid being _____ about her situation.

4) Question her _____ on abortion:
   - What prompted you to call about your problem?
   - What are your real feelings about abortion?
   - What have you heard from others, Christian or not regarding abortion?

26

5) Whether or not she believes abortion is wrong, present the <u>Scriptures</u> given in class along with any others that you think would apply.

6) Ask her to consider the _____.

7) If she is concerned about not being able to care for or support the child, ask her to consider _____.

8) Ask her if she has ever received Jesus Christ as her Lord and Savior. If appropriate, present the _____.

9) Suggest that she start reading the _____.

10) Ask if she has a _____ home. She should try to identify with a Bible-teaching church where she can find fellowship and encouragement, and can grow in her faith.

VII. The Woman Who Has Had an Abortion and Suffers from Guilt

1) Encourage her by saying that she has made the right choice in seeking help. We care and want to help in any way we can. God has an answer to every human situation, and she can trust Him to work for her good.

2) Don't make a moral issue of her situation; at the same time, don't minimize the seriousness of such a choice. The fact that she is willing to share her feelings of guilt is an indication that God is speaking to her.

3) Dwell on God's forgiveness for those who are willing to repent and confess their sins to the Lord. To the woman taken in the act of adultery, Jesus said, "Neither do I condemn you; go and sin no more" (John 8: 11).

4) Should confession result, do not dwell on the past (Philippians 3: 13-14).

5) Ask if she has ever received Jesus Christ as her personal Savior. If appropriate, present the gospel.

6) Suggest that she seek fellowship with God through Bible reading and prayer. Forgiveness is immediate, but a sense of restoration and acceptance will come in due time. Through commitment to this important discipline of prayer and Bible study, she will grow in her relationship with God.

7) Suggest that she seek, or restore, fellowship with a Bible-teaching church. There she can counsel with a pastor, hear God's Word taught, and find strength through Christian relationships.

8) Pray with her. Ask God for forgiveness, commitment, and strength for the future.

Selected Scriptures for Healing

- Anger - Ephesians 4:26, 31-32; Hebrews 12:15

- Depression - Psalm 40:1-5, 8-17; Psalm 6

- Forgiveness - Psalm 32:1-5; Psalm 51:1-3; 1 John 1:9; 2 Corinthians 5:21; Colossians 3:12-13

- Peace - Colossians 3:15; Matthew 11:28-30; Isaiah 26:3-4

- Support - Galatians 6:1-2; Psalm 27

- Perseverance - Hebrews 12:1-2; Galatians 2:20; 1 Corinthians 6:11; Philippians 3:13-14

CSER Opportunities - The Liberty Godparent Home & Blue Ridge Pregnancy Center

EUTHANASIA

How valuable is human life?

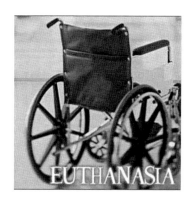

What does the Bible say about Euthanasia?

Deuteronomy 5:17 (NLT) - *Do not murder.*

Job 1:21 (NKJV) - *And he said: "Naked I came from my mother's womb, And naked shall I return there. The Lord gave, and the Lord has taken away; Blessed be the name of the Lord."*

2 Corinthians 12:9 (NKJV) *And He said to me, "My grace is sufficient for you, for My strength is made perfect in weakness." Therefore most gladly I will rather boast in my infirmities, that the power of Christ may rest upon me.*

The term euthanasia is derived from the Greek prefix <u>eu</u>, meaning "_____" and the Greek noun <u>thanatos</u>, meaning "_____." Today the word is used to denote the act of one person killing another because the person killed is terminally ill, suffering, disabled, or elderly.

I. Euphemisms

- "Death with _____"
- "Dying Gracefully"
- "Compassion in Dying"
- "Planned Death"
- "_____ Death"

II. Prominent Names to Know

Derek Humphrey – head of the Hemlock Society (now named "Compassion and Choices"

Jack Kevorkian – Dr. Death

Karen Ann Quinlan – was on a respirator and feeding tube, in a persistent vegetative state, taken off life support in 1976 after the New Jersey Supreme Court allowed the respirator to be removed because of the "right to privacy". Karen lived 10 more years.

Terry Schiavo – suffered severe brain damage in 1990 and finally taken off life support and feeding tube in 2005 and died

_____ – first nation to legalize euthanasia and even child euthanasia
(Also legal in Belgium, Albania, Luxembourg, also in Switzerland – not legal, but not punished)

How about in the United States?

III. Types of Euthanasia

Is there such a thing as the "_____ to die"?

Should we consider "_____ of life" over "_____ of life"?

1. _____ Euthanasia

Withholding medical treatment or discontinuing treatment ..."letting die"...cause of death is the same as the condition causing the suffering (disease, respiratory failure, etc).

  Is this truly euthanasia?

2. _____ Euthanasia

Actively doing something to bring about the death of the patient...lethal injection, smothering with a pillow, etc....the cause of death is not the condition causing the suffering, but rather something else.

3. _____ Euthanasia

Occurs when a patient explicitly refuses to be killed, and his or her request is not honored.

4. _____ Euthanasia

Occurs when a patient is killed by someone who is not aware of the patient's wishes, either because those wishes are unobtainable or because the person chooses not to obtain them.

5. _____ Euthanasia

Patient requests his/her own death - either verbally, in writing or via a living will. (Some states will recognize testimony of family/friends, but not all)

6. _____ Suicide

This is a suicide in which a person's reasons for dying are similar to that of euthanasia. However, rather than take his or her own life, the person is assisted in the suicide by a physician.

For further information, see Stewart, Gary: *Basic Questions on Suicide and Euthanasia : Are They Ever Right?*. Grand Rapids, MI : Kregel Publicationi, 1998 (BioBasics Series).

IV. Five Main Arguments Used To Promote Euthanasia

- ■_____
- ■_____
- ■_____
- ■_____
- ■_____
- ■_____

V. Commonly Used Defenses For Euthanasia

- ■It is a religious issue

- Guidelines can prevent uses/abuses

- It would only be for the "_____ _____"

- We euthanize _____ to relieve suffering, why not people?

- There is no difference between "choice" in _____ and "choice" in euthanasia

VI. Consequences

- When life is _____, it slowly depreciates further over time

- _____ of Life Ethic is replacing a _____ of Life Ethic

- A _____ to die will eventually be transformed into a _____ to die

- The power to choose will broaden from the _____ to the "_____" to those "_____ invested" to "_____" and so on.

- Options will become less available

- Expanding _____ inevitable

VII. Traditional Arguments Against Euthanasia

1. Expanding Expendability

2. Physician/Patient relationship will weaken

3. Quality of life ethic leads to some lives being deemed more _____ than others

4. _____ of the process & guidelines

5. Diagnoses and prognoses may be wrong

6. There will become a _____ to die

7. Violation of the _____ Oath

A slippery slope?
Terminally ill
Chronically ill
Depressed
Newborns with birth defects

VIII. Biblical View of Euthanasia

1. Man is created in the _____ of God.

   Then God said, "Let us make man in our image, in our likeness, and let them rule over the fish of the sea and the birds of the air, over the livestock, over all the earth, and over all the creatures that move along the ground." – Genesis 1:26. See also Genesis 9:6.

2. Human life is _____ and should not be terminated merely because it is difficult.

3. God is _____ over life and death.

   See now that I myself am He! There is no god besides me. I put to death and I bring to life, I have wounded and I will heal, and no one can deliver out of my hand. – Deuteronomy 32:39. See also Job 1:21; Psalm 139:16; Ecclesiastes 3:1-2.

4. The Bible specifically condemns the taking of life.

   You must not murder – Exodus 20:13.

5. We are responsible to care for the _____ and innocent.

   Learn to do good. Seek justice. Help the oppressed. Defend the cause of orphans. Fight for the rights of widows – Isaiah 1:17. See also Deuteronomy 14:29; Job 22:9.

6. Our _____ as well as our spirit belongs to God.

   Don't you realize that your body is the temple of the Holy Spirit, who lives in you and was given to you by God? You do not belong to yourself, for God bought you with a high price. So you must honor God with your body – 1 Corinthians 6:19-20.

7. God has a purpose for everything even when we don't understand that purpose.

   And we know that in all things God works for the good of those who love him, who have been called according to his purpose – Romans 8:28. See also Romans 11:33.

8. _____ has a place in God's economy

   (Blessed be the God and Father of our Lord Jesus Christ, the Father of mercies and God of all comfort, who comforts us in all our affliction, so that we may be able to comfort those who are in any affliction, with the comfort with which we ourselves are comforted by God. For as we share abundantly in Christ's sufferings, so through Christ we share abundantly in comfort too. If we are afflicted, it is for your comfort and salvation; and if we are comforted, it is for your comfort, which you experience when you patiently endure the same sufferings that we suffer. Our hope for you is unshaken, for we know that as you share in our sufferings, you will also share in our comfort. – 2 Corinthians 1:3-7.

9. As a result of the fall, death is _____.

Therefore, just as sin entered the world through one man, and death through sin, and in this way death came to all men, because all sinned – Romans 5:12. See also Romans 6:23.

IX. What Is Hospice?

- Help patients and families deal with the fear of the _____.

- Help with _____ control.

- Thoughts of suicide and depression are dealt with.

- They deal with the "_____" issue.

- They help the family deal with the _____ of the dying.

X. What Can We Do?

- Be Informed.

    o Inform populace of alternatives.

    o Inform people of the dangers of "_____ the door".

    o Train doctors in _____ management.

- Be Involved.

- Be In Touch

CSER Opportunities to work with the Elderly

CSER 501-01: CAMELOT HALL OF LYNCHBURG

CSER 504-01: AREA AGENCY ON AGING

CSER 505-01: WESTMINSTER CANTERBURY

CSER 514-01: THE OAKS OF LYNCHBURG

CSER 524-01: THE CARRINGTON

CSER 527-01: ADULT CARE CENTER

CSER 544-01: CARRIAGE HILL ASSISTED CARE

CSER 545-01: LYNCHBURG PARKS AND RECREATION

CSER 557-01: RUNK & PRATT RESIDENTIAL CARE

CSER 568-001: HERITAGE GREEN/DAYBREAK (FORMERLY MAYFAIR HOUSE)

GENDER ISSUES

What are some differences in men and women?

What are some stereotypes?

What are some of the gender problems that we face in our society today?

What Does The Bible Say About Gender?

Proverbs 31:10 (KJV) - Who can find a virtuous woman? For her price is far above rubies. (Just read the whole chapter!)

Ephesians 5:24-25 (NET) - But as the church submits to Christ, so also wives should submit to their husbands in everything. Husbands, love your wives just as Christ loved the church and gave himself for her

Acts 18:26 (NIV) - When Priscilla and Aquila heard him preaching boldly in the synagogue, they took him aside and explained the way of God even more accurately.

<u>**Two evangelical responses to the gender debates:**</u>

1. Egalitarianism (Biblical Feminism)

"Gender equity", "gender equality", "sexual equality", or **gender egalitarianism** is the belief in the equality of the gender or the sexes.

The belief and interpretive framework that attempts to apply basic feminist ideas of equality to the Scriptures and thus the home and church. While rejecting the extremes of feminism, like an androgynous society, the tendency is to interpret Scripture as a "patriarchal" book limited to its time and culture. It focuses on the new ways in which women were being viewed and treated by Jesus and even suggested by Paul as totally equal to men in every way and not to be limited in terms of any ministry opportunities by their gender – Will Honeycutt

2. Complementarianism

A view of the relationship between the genders that differs from egalitarianism, in that it believes that both men and women are equal in status, but can have different and *complementary* roles.

A response to biblical feminism to reaffirm that men and women are equal in essence or identity having been created in the image of God, but still have differing roles in the home and church based on gender distinctions created by God. With regard to these roles, in the home the man is to be the loving head of the woman, and the woman is to voluntarily submit to his leadership. In the church, God has ordained that men are to lead the church, and women are to support this work in the use of their gifts. There are God-ordained roles according to gender, and it is in fulfilling them that both men and women will find their greatest fulfillment in life – Will Honeycutt

I. Men and Women in Society – Genesis 1:26-28

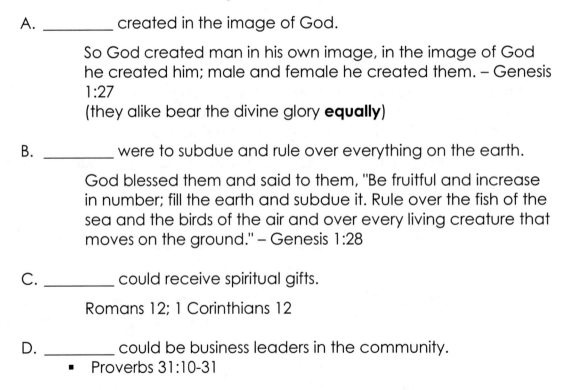

A. _____ created in the image of God.

> So God created man in his own image, in the image of God he created him; male and female he created them. – Genesis 1:27
> (they alike bear the divine glory **equally**)

B. _____ were to subdue and rule over everything on the earth.

> God blessed them and said to them, "Be fruitful and increase in number; fill the earth and subdue it. Rule over the fish of the sea and the birds of the air and over every living creature that moves on the ground." – Genesis 1:28

C. _____ could receive spiritual gifts.

Romans 12; 1 Corinthians 12

D. _____ could be business leaders in the community.
- Proverbs 31:10-31

- There is NO reason why a woman cannot be a CEO, etc.
- There is NO reason why women shouldn't receive <u>equal</u> pay.

E. _____ are spiritually equal in Christ.

> There is neither Jew nor Greek, slave nor free, male nor female, for you are all one in Christ Jesus. – Galatians 3:28

Key Scriptures: 1 Corinthians 11:3-16; Ephesians 5:21-33; 1 Timothy 2:11-14.

> **Different roles** are traced back to creation, not the fall of man. Leadership and submission have nothing to do with superiority and inferiority.

II. Men and Women in the Home – Genesis 2:18-25

A. The role of the husband

- _____ his wife and sacrifice for her.

  Husbands, love your wives, just as Christ loved the church and gave himself up for her – Ephesians 5:25.
  Also see Colossians 3:19.

- _____ of the wife.

  For the husband is the head of the wife as Christ is the head of the church, his body, of which he is the Savior. 24Now as the church submits to Christ, so also wives should submit to their husbands in everything – Ephesians 5:23-24.
  Also see Titus 2:5, 1 Corinthians 11:3 (not male domination).

- Provide for his family.

  If anyone does not provide for his relatives, and especially for his immediate family, he has denied the faith and is worse than an unbeliever – 1 Timothy 5:8.

- _____ in the home.

- Honor and _____ his wife.

  Husbands, in the same way be considerate as you live with your wives, and treat them with respect as the weaker partner and as heirs with you of the gracious gift of life, so that nothing will hinder your prayers – 1 Peter 3:7.

- Provide a positive environment for <u>children</u>.

  Colossians 3:21.

B. **The role of the wife**

- Be a _____ to him.

  The LORD God said, "It is not good for the man to be alone. I will make a helper suitable for him." – Genesis 2:18.
  Also see v. 20.
  How should the wife be a helper to her husband?

- _____ to her husband, (not to men in general) - Ephesians 5:22-24; 1 Peter 3:1-6; 1 Corinthians 11:3 (not feminism).
  "The principle of subordination and authority pervades the entire universe. Paul shows that woman's subordination to man is but a reflection of that greater general truth. Christ is the head of every man, and the man is the head of a woman, and God is the head of Christ. If Christ had not submitted to the will of God, redemption for mankind would have been impossible, and we would forever be doomed and lost. If individual human beings do not submit to Christ as Savior and Lord, they are still doomed and lost, because they reject God's gracious provision. And if women do not submit to men, then the family and society as a whole are disrupted and destroyed. Whether on a divine or human scale, subordination and authority are indispensable elements in God's order and plan."
  (MacArthur, John F., 1 Corinthians: The MacArthur New Testament Commentary, (Chicago: Moody Press) 1984).

  What are some common, but biblically wrong views of submission?

- Love her husband and children.

  Then they (the older women) can train the younger women to love their husbands and children – Titus 2:4.

- Keep the family a _____.

  So I counsel younger widows to marry, to have children, to manage their homes and to give the enemy no opportunity for slander – 1 Timothy 5:14.
  Also see Titus 2:5.

C. **The reversal of roles** and the consequences - Genesis 3:17-19.

- A desire for the woman to _____ over the man – conflict.

- Curse upon the man for listening to the woman and abandoning his role of loving _____.

- The curse came because of what _____ did, not because of what _____ did.

- The death sentence was on Adam as the head, not Eve, but Eve still died, because as the head goes, so goes the helper.

III. A Woman's Role in the Church

A. **What women can do:**

1. _____ younger women - Older women likewise are to be reverent in behavior, not slanderers or slaves to much wine. They are to teach what is good, and so train the young women to love their husbands and children - Titus 2:3-4.

2. Teach children - I am reminded of your sincere faith, a faith that dwelt first in your grandmother Lois and your mother Eunice and now, I am sure, dwells in you as well. - 2 Timothy 1:5. See also 2 Timothy 3:15.

3. _____ - 1 Corinthians 11:5.

4. Sing - Colossians 3:16 (nothing gender specific - Note v. 18).

5. Correct _____ teaching - He began to speak boldly in the synagogue, but when Priscilla and Aquila heard him, they took him aside and explained to him the way of God more accurately. - Acts 18:26 (Aquila, Priscilla & Apollos).

6. Vote - Acts 1:14-26 (Women took part in voting for a replacement for Judas Iscariot).

7. Serve as Deaconess? - I commend to you our sister Phoebe, a servant of the church at Cenchreae, that you may welcome her in the Lord in a way worthy of the saints, and help her in whatever she may need from you, for she has been a patron of many and of myself as well. - Romans 16:1-2.

"Servant translates *diakonos*, the term from which we get deacon. The Greek word here is neuter and was used in the church as a general term for servant before the offices of deacon and deaconess were developed. It is used of the household servants who drew the water that Jesus turned into wine (John 2:5, 9), and Paul has used the term earlier in this letter (Rom. 13:4, twice) to refer to secular government as "a minister of God to you for good" and even of Christ as "a servant to the circumcision," that is, to Jews (15:8). When *diakonos* obviously refers to a church office, it is usually transliterated as "deacon" (see, e.g., Philippians 1:1; 1 Timothy 3:10, 13).

In 1 Timothy 3:11, Paul declares that "women must likewise be dignified, not malicious gossips, but temperate, faithful in all things." Some argue that he is referring to wives of deacons, rather than to an office of women deacons. But it makes no sense that high standards would be specified for the wives of deacons but not for wives of overseers (or bishops, who are also called elders, see Titus 1:5), whose qualifications he has just given in verses 1–7. In this context (3:1–10, 12–13), the office of deaconess is clearly implied. The "likewise" in verse 11 ties the qualifications of these women to those already given for the offices of overseer and deacon. In verse 11, Paul did not refer to those women as deaconesses because *diakonos* has no feminine form" - *(MacArthur, John F., Romans (volume 2): The MacArthur New Testament Commentary, (Chicago: Moody Press) 1994, p. 360).*

What other things can women do in the church?

B. **What women cannot do:**

1. _____ a church - Let a woman learn quietly with all submissiveness. I do not permit a woman to teach or to exercise authority over a man; rather, she is to remain quiet. For Adam was formed first, then Eve; and Adam was not deceived, but the woman was deceived and became a transgressor. - 1 Timothy 2:11-14. The saying is trustworthy: If anyone aspires to the office of overseer, he desires a noble task. Therefore an overseer must be above reproach, the husband of one wife, sober-minded, self-controlled, respectable, hospitable, able to teach 1 Timothy 3:1-2.

2. Teach and rule in _____ over a man. - 1 Timothy 2:11-14.

   Could a woman be a better preacher or shepherd than a man?

   Is it all right for a woman to speak from a church pulpit?

2:11 - Let a woman learn. Women are not to be the public teachers when the church assembles, but neither are they to be shut out of the learning process. The form of the Gr. verb translated "let ... learn" is an imperative: Paul is commanding that women be taught in the church. That was a novel concept, since neither first century Judaism nor Greek culture held women in high esteem.

2:12 - I do not permit. The Gr. word for "permit" is used in the NT to refer to allowing someone to do what he desires. Paul may have been addressing a real situation in which several women in Ephesus desired to be public preachers...Thus Paul is forbidding women from filling the office and role of the pastor or teacher. He is not prohibiting them from teaching in other appropriate conditions and circumstances (cf. Acts 18:26; Titus 2:3-4). **To have authority over.** Paul forbids women from exercising any type of authority over men in the church assembly, since the elders are those who rule (5:17). They are all to be men (as is clear from the requirements in 3:2, 5) - John MacArthur, Jr., The MacArthur Study Bible, p. 1863.

HOMOSEXUALITY

Do you know someone who is homosexual?

What does the Bible say about Homosexuality?
---

1. **Leviticus 18:22 (NLT)** - "Do not practice homosexuality; it is a detestable sin.

2. **Romans 1:26-27 (NIV)** Because of this, God gave them over to shameful lusts. Even their women exchanged natural relations for unnatural ones. In the same way the men also abandoned natural relations with women and were inflamed with lust for one another. Men committed indecent acts with other men, and received in themselves the due penalty for their perversion.

3. **1 Corinthians 6:9-11 (NET)** - Do you not know that the unrighteous will not inherit the kingdom of God? Do not be deceived! The sexually immoral, idolaters, adulterers, passive homosexual partners, practicing homosexuals, thieves, the greedy, drunkards, the verbally abusive, and swindlers will not inherit the kingdom of God. Some of you once lived this way. But you were washed, you were sanctified, you were justified in the name of the Lord Jesus Christ and by the Spirit of our God.

I. Homosexuality and the Bible

1. HOMOSEXUALITY WAS CONSIDERED A _____ IN THE DAYS OF THE PATRIARCHS.

   - Genesis 18:20 - Then the LORD said, "Because the outcry against Sodom and Gomorrah is great and their sin is very grave . . ."

     What was their sin?

   - Genesis 19:1-12 - Sodom and Gomorrah – Does this story give us greater insight?

   - Jude 7 - just as Sodom and Gomorrah and the surrounding cities, which likewise indulged in sexual immorality and pursued unnatural desire, serve as an example by undergoing a punishment of eternal fire.

2. HOMOSEXUALITY WAS CONSIDERED "A _____ CRIME" UNDER THE MOSAIC LAW.

    - Leviticus 18:22 - "abomination" or "detestable"

    - Leviticus 20:13 - If a man lies with a male as with a woman, both of them have committed an abomination; they shall surely be put to death; their blood is upon them.

    - Note: Moral laws and ceremonial laws

3. THE NEW TESTAMENT IS CLEAR IN ITS _____ OF HOMOSEXUAL CONDUCT

    - 1 Corinthians 6:9-11 – Or do you not know that the unrighteous will not inherit the kingdom of God? Do not be deceived: neither the sexually immoral, nor idolaters, nor adulterers, nor men who practice homosexuality, nor thieves, nor the greedy, nor drunkards, nor revilers, nor swindlers will inherit the kingdom of God. And such were some of you. But you were washed, you were sanctified, you were justified in the name of the Lord Jesus Christ and by the Spirit of our God.

        Homosexuality is in a list of sins, sins that can be forgiven by Christ, but still considered to be sins.

        The phrase "men who practice homosexuality" translates two Greek terms that refer to both the passive and active partners in consensual homosexual activities.

    - Romans 1:24-32 - Therefore God gave them up in the lusts of their hearts to impurity, to the dishonoring of their bodies among themselves, because they exchanged the truth about God for a lie and worshiped and served the creature rather than the Creator, who is blessed forever! Amen. For this reason God gave them up to dishonorable passions. For their women exchanged natural relations for those that are contrary to nature; and the men likewise gave up natural relations with women and were consumed with passion for one another, men committing shameless acts with men and receiving in themselves the due penalty for their error. And since they did not see fit to acknowledge God, God gave them up to a debased mind to do what ought not to be done. (vv. 24-28)

    - 1 Timothy 1:8-10 - Now we know that the law is good, if one uses it lawfully, understanding this, that the law is not laid down for the just but for the lawless and disobedient, for the ungodly and sinners, for the unholy and profane, for those who strike their fathers and mothers, for murderers, the sexually immoral, men who practice homosexuality, enslavers, liars, perjurers, and whatever else is contrary to sound doctrine.

II.   Important Things to Know About Homosexuality

1. The 2010 United States Census determined that there are 131,729 married same-sex couples in America.

2. It also shows that there are 514,735 same-sex unmarried couples in America.

3. It is estimated that somewhere between 1½-3% of the population may be gay in some sense.

4. Important terms to understand (taken from The Meaning of Sex by Dennis Hollinger

    - Homosexual orientation – "refers to the reality that a small percentage of human beings have ongoing affectional and sexual feelings toward persons of the same sex."

    - Homosexual identity – "refers to the self-perception wherein the core of one's being and the shape of one's life is defined by homosexuality." A person is not born with this identity, but shapes it through the groups he/she is in or the experiences he/she has. It is a choice.

    - Homosexual behavior – "is the acting out of one's homosexual impulses in physical intimacy with a person of the same sex." This is a matter of choice.

    - Thus, the ethical issue is not about orientation, but about identity and behavior.

III.   Myths About Homosexuality

According to information from the Family Research Council

1. People are born gay

    - Research shows no real evidence of this

2. Sexual orientation can never change

- Thousands of men and women have changed though from homosexual to heterosexual

3. Efforts to change someone's sexual orientation from homosexual to heterosexual are harmful and unethical

   - There is no scientific evidence of this

4. Ten percent of the population is gay

   - As we have already seen, this is not the case

5. Homosexuals do not experience a higher level of psychological disorders than heterosexuals

   - Studies have shown that there is a greater level of mental illness and substance abuse

6. Homosexual conduct is not harmful to one's physical health

   - There is more sexual promiscuity and physical harm and injury to the body and greater risk of sexually transmitted diseases

7. Children raised by homosexuals are no different from children raised by heterosexuals, nor do they suffer harm

   - Studies show that children raised by mother and father who are committed to one another do best, but not all studies are complete yet

8. Homosexuals are no more likely to molest children than heterosexuals

   - This especially applies to men. Most pedophiles are men. This does not say that most homosexuals are child molesters, but the rate of child sexual abuse among homosexuals is higher than it is among heterosexuals.

9. Homosexuals are seriously disadvantaged by discrimination

   - They actually have higher levels of educational attainment. This is not to deny that there is discrimination in some ways.

10. Homosexual relationships are just the same as heterosexual ones, except for the gender of the partners

    - Commitment is less likely, sexual faithfulness to one person is less likely, and domestic violence is more likely

IV. The Homosexual View of Bible Passages.

1. The sin of Sodom was not homosexuality but _____. This is due to the interpretation of the Hebrew word "yada". - Genesis 19:5 - And they

called to Lot, "Where are the men who came to you tonight? Bring them out to us, that we may know them."

2. Some believe _____ and _____ were gay lovers. See I Samuel 18-20 - key verses: 18:3-4 - Then Jonathan made a covenant with David, because he loved him as his own soul. And Jonathan stripped himself of the robe that was on him and gave it to David, and his armor, and even his sword and his bow and his belt.

   20:41 - And as soon as the boy had gone, David rose from beside the stone heap and fell on his face to the ground and bowed three times. And they kissed one another and wept with one another, David weeping the most.

   2 Samuel 1:26 - I am distressed for you, my brother Jonathan; very pleasant have you been to me; your love to me was extraordinary, surpassing the love of women.

3. 1 Corinthians 6:9 only speaks against offenses i.e. improper homosexual activity. It says, Or do you not know that the unrighteous will not inherit the kingdom of God? Do not be deceived: neither the sexually immoral, nor idolaters, nor adulterers, nor men who practice homosexuality . . .

Two Christian groups that promote homosexuality as biblical are Soul Force led by Mel White and a group of churches across the nation known as the Metropolitan Community Church.

V. A Christian Approach to Homosexuality

1. SPEAK THE _____ IN _____

   - Rather, speaking the truth in love, we are to grow up in every way into him who is the head, into Christ (Ephesians 4:15)

   - "And a servant of the Lord must not quarrel but be gentle to all, able to teach, patient, in humility correcting those who are in opposition, if God perhaps will grant them repentance, so that they may know the truth, and that they may come to their senses and escape the snare of the devil, having been taken captive by him to do his will." (2 Timothy 2:24-26).

2. HOMOSEXUALITY IS A _____ PATTERN THAT CAN BE CHANGED

   - "Do not be deceived: Neither the sexually immoral nor idolaters nor adulterers nor male prostitutes nor homosexual offenders... will inherit the kingdom of God. And that is what some of you were. But you were washed, you were sanctified, you were justified in the name of the Lord Jesus Christ and by the Spirit of our God" - 1 Corinthians 6:9-11.

3. _____ THOSE WHO WANT TO OVERCOME HOMOSEXUALITY

- "Brethren, if a man is overtaken in any trespass, you who are spiritual restore such a one in a spirit of gentleness, considering yourself lest you also be tempted. Bear one another's burdens, and so fulfill the law of Christ." - (Galatians 6:1-2).

A Biblical Model of Homosexuality

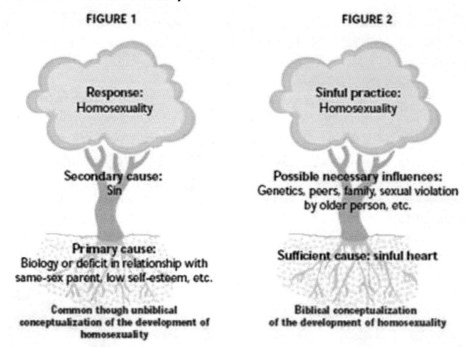

FIGURE 1

Response:
Homosexuality

Secondary cause:
Sin

Primary cause:
Biology or deficit in relationship with same-sex parent, low self-esteem, etc.

Common though unbiblical conceptualization of the development of homosexuality

FIGURE 2

Sinful practice:
Homosexuality

Possible necessary influences:
Genetics, peers, family, sexual violation by older person, etc.

Sufficient cause: sinful heart

Biblical conceptualization of the development of homosexuality

http://www.afa.net

What should be my attitude toward Homosexuality?
(Taken from: The Moral Catastrophe by David Hocking)

1. Do not _____ homosexuals; hate homosexuality and what it does to people.

2. Never believe that "sexual preferences" should be added to our understanding and application of _____ or civil rights.

3. Do not discriminate against homosexuals in terms of the rights to which all Americans are entitled, but never be intimidated or pressured to _____ or _____ their lifestyle and activity.

4. Teach your children what the _____ says about sexual matters, and warn them of sexual sins (adultery, homosexuality etc)

5. Do not treat homosexuality as a more terrible sin than adultery among heterosexuals, but never view it as harmless or tolerable.

6. Encourage homosexuals to accept God's _____ and _____ in the work and person of Jesus Christ. Show them that God's power can give them the inner strength, courage, and desire not to be involved in homosexual activities.

7. Make sure that your own personal beliefs, principles and lifestyle are in line with biblical morality. You should be committed to demonstrating that the only _____ and _____ sex is between a husband and a wife.

Christian/Community Service Applications

While a Community service assignment may not entail specifically ministering to homosexuals it is possible that students may have opportunity to address this contemporary issue in a variety of Christian/Community service contexts.

What would you do if you encountered someone from the group Soul Force or someone from a Metropolitan Community Church?

What impact should this chapter have on the way you speak about or treat those who are gay? Be very practical and very specific.

DATING RELATIONSHIPS

Did you date while you were in high school?

Are you dating now?

How should your worldview affect your dating relationships?

What does the Bible say about Dating?

1. **2 Corinthians 6:14-15 (NET)** - Do not become partners with those who do not believe, for what partnership is there between righteousness and lawlessness, or what fellowship does light have with darkness? And what agreement does Christ have with Beliar? Or what does a believer share in common with an unbeliever?

2. **1 Thessalonians 4:3-5 (ESV)** - For this is the will of God, your sanctification: that you abstain from sexual immorality; that each one of you know how to control his own body in holiness and honor, not in the passion of lust like the Gentiles who do not know God;

3. **2 Timothy 2:22 (NIV)** - Flee the evil desires of youth, and pursue righteousness, faith, love and peace, along with those who call on the Lord out of a pure heart.

<u>The Three BIGGEST Decisions of Your Life</u>

- Who is my _____?

- What is my _____?

- Who is my _____?

I.   Dating Defined

1. A form of romantic courtship between two individuals who may or may not expect marriage. www.allwords.com

2. An engagement to go out socially with another person, often out of romantic interest. www.freedictionary.com

3. Dating is a stage in a relationship in which the two individuals involved get acquainted by doing activities together. Causal dating is the process in which people meet and go out together without any expectation of a long-term, committed relationship. When two people are casually dating, they are usually spending time together without an exclusive relationship or any agreement to date in the future. – www.ehow.com

4. The process of spending enormous amounts of money, time, and energy to get better acquainted with a person whom you do not especially like now, but will learn to like a lot less.

5. A prearranged social activity shared by two _____ persons of the _____ sex.

• *What are some good reasons to date?*

II.   Types of Dating

• Recreational or casual dating involves a relationship that revolves around an event. There is no _____ beyond the date.

• Attachment-oriented dating or serious dating involves some level of commitment. Dating revolves around their _____ rather than the event.

III.   Purposes of Dating

• Recreation (is this good? Why or why not?)

• To provide opportunities to serve others

• To learn to listen

- To get to know those of the opposite sex and to learn to relate to them as persons made in the image of God

- To learn to see others as persons, not objects

- To enable one to learn more about oneself, including strengths and weaknesses

- _____ socialization for marriage and family roles

- To facilitate _____ selection, discover the kind of person you will marry

See article by Gary Chapman - http://www.crosswalk.com/1302909/

What are some wrong reasons to date?

Seven Habits of Highly Defective Dating

(Taken from Joshua Harris - I Kissed Dating Goodbye)

1. Dating leads to _____ but not necessarily to commitment.

2. Dating tends to skip the "_____" stage of a relationship.

3. Dating often mistakes a _____ relationship for _____.

4. Dating often _____ a couple from other vital relationships.

5. Dating, in many cases, distracts young adults from their primary responsibility of preparing for the future.

6. Dating can cause discontentment with God's gift of singleness. (a string of uncommitted relationships is not a gift).

7. Dating creates an artificial environment for evaluating another person's character.

IV. The Priority For Dating – <u>PURITY</u>

1. The Bible does not even mention "dating"

2. Dating was not common until recent centuries and is still not common in many parts of the world

3. Purity is the highest priority in relationships

1) "In the general sense common to the NT, and to the devotional literature of the OT, purity indicates a state of heart where there is complete devotion to God." New Bible Dictionary, p. 991

2) "In the specialized sense purity came to mean freedom from sensual pollution, particularly in the sexual life, though the NT does not teach that sexual activity is polluting in itself and, indeed, makes it clear that rightly ordered sexual behavior is not . . . Purity is thus the spirit of renunciation and of the obedience which brings every thought and feeling and action into subjection to Christ. It begins within and extends outwards to the entire life, cleansing all the centers of living and controlling all the movements of body and spirit." New Bible Dictionary, 991

3) Inner and outer purity are required

✓ 1 Corinthians 7:1 - Now concerning the matters about which you wrote: "It is good for a man not to have sexual relations with a woman." (What does the passage say after verse 1?)

✓ Romans 13:13-14 - Let us walk properly as in the daytime, not in orgies and drunkenness, not in sexual immorality and sensuality, not in quarreling and jealousy. But put on the Lord Jesus Christ, and make no provision for the flesh, to gratify its desires.

✓ 1 Corinthians 6:13b - The body is not meant for sexual immorality, but for the Lord, and the Lord for the body.

✓ 1 Corinthians 6:18-19 - Flee from sexual immorality. Every other sin a person commits is outside the body, but the sexually immoral person sins against his own body. Or do you not know that your body is a temple of the Holy Spirit within you, whom you have from God? You are not your own, for you were bought with a price. So glorify God in your body.

✓ 1 Timothy 1:5 - The aim of our charge is love that issues from a pure heart and a good conscience and a sincere faith.

✓ 2 Timothy 2:22 - So flee youthful passions and pursue righteousness, faith, love, and peace, along with those who call on the Lord from a pure heart.

✓ 1 Thessalonians 4:3 - For this is the will of God, your sanctification: that you abstain from sexual immorality.

4) *What will purity look like in a dating relationship?*

5) *What are you doing to make purity a priority in your life?*

6) *Is pornography a part of your life? See Job 31:1!*

7) A warning and a promise – 1 Corinthians 10:12-13 - Therefore let anyone who thinks that he stands take heed lest he fall. No temptation has overtaken you that is not common to man. God is faithful, and he will not let you be tempted beyond your ability, but with the temptation he will also provide the way of escape, that you may be able to endure it.

V.   Pitfalls of Dating

Why do dating relationships so easily lead to sexual relationships?

1. When the _____ aspect is dominant, the social, intellectual, and spiritual elements of the relationship will suffer.

2. The possibility of becoming too _____ too fast.

   (Friendship, Dating, Engagement, Marriage)

3. Reputation – Proverbs 22:1 - A good name is to be chosen rather than great riches, and favor is better than silver or gold. 2 Corinthians 6:14.

4. Spiritual condition – 2 Corinthians 6:14 - Do not be unequally yoked with unbelievers. For what partnership has righteousness with lawlessness? Or what fellowship has light with darkness? 1 Corinthians 5:11.

5. Flesh control.

   – _____

   James 1:14-16 - But each person is tempted when he is lured and enticed by his own desire. Then desire when it has conceived gives birth to sin, and sin when it is fully grown brings forth death. Do not be deceived, my beloved brothers.

   When does lust begin?

– _____

1 Timothy 2:9-10 - likewise also that women should adorn themselves in respectable apparel, with modesty and self-control, not with braided hair and gold or pearls or costly attire, but with what is proper for women who profess godliness—with good works.

What is modest?

What is not?

How Far is too Far In A Dating Relationship? - Is it?:

1. All the Way (1 Corinthians 6:9-11)

2. When it becomes _____ (1 Thessalonians 4:3-9)

3. When one feels _____ (Romans 14:13-23)

Where will you draw the line?

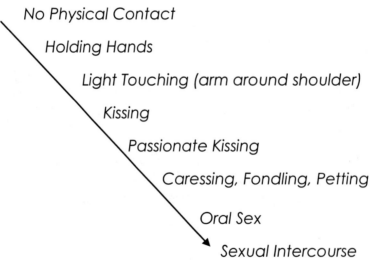

No Physical Contact

Holding Hands

Light Touching (arm around shoulder)

Kissing

Passionate Kissing

Caressing, Fondling, Petting

Oral Sex

Sexual Intercourse

What kind of commitment is required to draw the proper line and then live by that commitment?

A commitment to _____

10 Ways to Practice Purity
(Campus Life – Jan/Feb 2001)

1. Keep innocent expressions innocent.

(Rather than making innocent expressions a mere prelude to "heavier stuff").

2. Pace your passion.

(Realize you are trying to remain _____ all the way to your _____ day).

3. Don't feed _____.

   (Feeding your thought life with junk only makes it harder to remain pure).

4. Remember whose _____ you're touching.

   (That person belongs to _____).

5. Make a _____ to God, and daily renew your commitment.

   (Seek God and draw the line, then keep it).

6. Acknowledge Jesus' presence on every date.

   (Start & finish your date with _____ – _____ take leadership).

7. Agree on your _____.

   (Talk about your standards/line together).

8. Don't always go it alone.

   (Be selective where – Spend time with others).

9. Put real love first. (always _____) – See 1 Corinthians 13.

10. Declare a new beginning. (start now).

VI. Biblical Principles to Apply When Dating (www.bibleinfo.com)

1. What kind of person should you date?

   2 Timothy 2:22 (TLB) - "Run from anything that gives you the evil thoughts that young men often have, but stay close to anything that makes you want to do right. Have faith and love, and enjoy the companionship of those who love the Lord and have pure hearts."

2. Don't date someone who doesn't _____ God.

2 Corinthians 6:14-15 (TLB) - *"Don't be teamed with those who do not love the Lord, for what do the people of God have in common with the people of sin? How can light live with darkness? How can a Christian be a partner with one who doesn't believe?"* - Amos 3:3 - *"Can two walk together, unless they are agreed?"*

3. Don't date someone who claims to be a Christian but doesn't _____ it.

    1 Corinthians 5:11 (TLB) - *"What I meant was that you are not to keep company with anyone who claims to be a brother Christian but indulges in sexual sins, or is greedy, or is a swindler, or worships idols, or is a drunkard, or abusive."*

4. _____ beauty counts the most.

    1 Peter 3:4 (TLB) - *"Be beautiful inside, in your hearts, with the lasting charm of a gentle and quiet spirit that is so precious to God."*

5. In a dating relationship don't be exclusive--care about others too.

    Philippians 2:4 (TLB) - *"Don't just think about your own affairs, but be interested in others, too, and in what they are doing."*

6. Let the relationship progress step by step.

    2 Peter 1:6-7 (TLB) - *"Next, learn to put aside your own desires so that you will become patient and godly, gladly letting God have his way with you. This will make possible the next step, which is for you to enjoy other people and to like them, and finally you will grow to love them deeply."*

7. What to avoid on dates.

    Romans 13:13 (TLB) - *"Be decent and true in everything you do so that all can approve your behavior. Don't spend your time in wild parties and getting drunk or in adultery and lust, or fighting, or jealousy."*

8. Dating should not include a _____ relationship.

    1 Corinthians 6:13, 18, TLB. *"But sexual sin is never right: our bodies were not made for that, but for the Lord . . .That is why I say to run from sex sin. No other sin affects the body as this one does. When you sin this sin it is against your own body."*

    1 Thessalonians 4:3-5, TLB. *"For God wants you to be holy and pure and to keep clear of all sexual sin so that each of you will marry in holiness and honor--not in lustful passion as the heathen do, in their ignorance of God and his ways."*

VII.   Dating, Immoral Sex & Its Consequences

<u>Hebrews 13:4</u> (NIV) - Marriage should be honored by all, and the marriage bed kept pure, for God will judge the adulterer and all the sexually immoral.

- ✓ God values _____.

- ✓ Sex in marriage is morally _____.

- ✓ Sexual relations outside marriage are _____.

CDC Releases Report on Sexual Behavior and Drug Use

Sunday, June 24, 2007
FOX NEWS

According to the <u>U.S. Centers for Disease Control and Prevention</u>, 96 percent of Americans over the age of 20 have had sex.

This is just one of the findings in a report issued Friday by the CDC's National Center for Health Statistics about American's sexual behavior and drug use.

The report uses data collected from 1999 to 2002 from 6,237 people aged 20 to 59. Participants submitted computer-assisted self-interviews about the use of cocaine, crack, freebase, and other street drugs, but marijuana was not included. Sexual behavior was defined as vaginal, oral or anal sex.

In previous federal surveys on these topics, participants were asked questions in face-to-face interviews; the CDC believes that caused underreporting of behaviors that might be viewed negatively.

"This is the first time we've used this technique," said Dr. Kathryn Porter, who served as medical officer for the survey. "The participants have a headset on, they hear questions, they touch the screen with responses. There's no one else in the room and they can take as long as they want."

Porter said the findings would provide grist for further studies, notably on the prevalence and patterns of sexually transmitted diseases.

Highlights from the report include:

• Twenty-nine percent of men reported 15 or more female sexual partners in a lifetime compared with 9 percent of women who reported having 15 or more male sexual partners in a lifetime.

• Of all race or ethnic groups, Mexican Americans had the highest percentage of persons never having sex at almost 12 percent.

• Sixteen percent of adults first had sex before the age of 15.

• Only 6 percent of non-Hispanic black persons abstained from sex until age 21 years and older compared with 17 percent for Mexican Americans and 15 percent for non-Hispanic white persons.

• The proportion of adults who first had sex before the age of 15 was highest for persons with less than a high school education

• The median number of lifetime female sexual partners for men was seven and the median number of lifetime male sexual partners for women was four.

Another CDC report from 2011 reports a survey of U.S. high school students:

47.4% had ever had sexual intercourse

33.7% had had sexual intercourse during the previous 3 months

15.3% had had sex with four or more people during their life

CONSEQUENCES

1) Physical – Proverbs 5:11; 1 Corinthians 6:18

   ✓ Unplanned _____

   ✓ _____

   ✓ Sexually transmitted diseases (_____)

   Estimated 65 million cases of STDs in the U.S.
   19 million new cases in 2010 according to the CDC
   17 billion annually in health care costs
   80 percent **of all female-factor infertility** is believed to be
   caused by untreated sexually transmitted diseases that have
   scarred fallopian tubes or caused damage to the
   reproductive tract. In fact, **one-third of all infertile women
   have had an abortion at some point in their lives.** (M. Sara
   Rosenthal, *The Fertility Sourcebook*, 3rd edition Chicago:
   Contemporary Books, 2002.)

   Bacterial – _____ with antibiotics, but can be dangerous

   - **Chlamydia** – Most common among teens (13-18), can lead
     to Pelvic Inflammatory Disease (PID), which in turn can
     cause dangerous tubal-pregnancies and/or result in
     infertility.
   - **Syphilis** – Can be transmitted through kissing because sores
     often appear in mouth. Can cause blindness, heart failure
     and brain damage. Has caused birth defects in children
     born to syphilitic parents.
   - **Gonorrhea** – Is increasing significantly among adolescents
     15-24.
   - **Trichomoniasis** – a parasite – 7.4 million new cases annually

   Viral – _____; can only be treated symptomatically.

   - **Genital Herpes** – About 1 million cases per year.
   - **Hepatitis B** – Most common cause of liver cancer in U.S.
     Transmitted to newborns, may be terminal.
   - **Human** Papillomavirus **(HPV)** –Most common STD among
     college-aged adults (18-29). Causes genital warts, and
     most cases of cervical cancer. Condoms generally do not
     protect against HPV. 20 million cases - 6.2 million new cases
     annually

- **HIV/AIDS** – Now the 6th leading cause of death among 15-20 year olds. Young women are the fastest growing group of HIV carriers (CDC, Atlanta, 1994), and HIV is spreading among lesbians (Planned Parenthood)

What about _____ and "_____" sex?

- 10-14% fail

- Latex is sensitive to heat and cold

- Latex has naturally occurring tiny holes or pores which generally block human sperm, but will not block HIV virus, Hepatitis B, Chlamydia, HPV, and Gonorrhea

- Dormant and undetected STDs -

2) Emotional – Sex is more than a physical act – 1 Corinthians 6:16

   ✓ _____ – Proverbs 5:11-14 - and at the end of your life you groan, when your flesh and body are consumed, and you say, "How I hated discipline, and my heart despised reproof! I did not listen to the voice of my teachers or incline my ear to my instructors. I am at the brink of utter ruin in the assembled congregation."

   ✓ Unwanted memories – Psalm 51:3 - For I know my transgressions, and my sin is ever before me.

   ✓ Feeling "dirty"

   ✓ Anxiety and _____

   ✓ Fear of _____

   ✓ Comparing sexual partners

   ✓ Anguish of unwanted _____

3) Spiritual/Moral – 1 Peter 2:11 - Beloved, I urge you as sojourners and exiles to abstain from the passions of the flesh, which wage war against your soul.

   ✓ Weakened _____ and moral resolve

   ✓ _____ from God – 1 Corinthians 6:9-10

✓ Hindrance to fruitfulness in the Christian life

✓ Less effective _____

4) Social – someone always pays

✓ Unwanted, unloved _____

✓ _____ of dollars for medical costs and treatment of STDs

✓ Abortions and their consequences (i.e. depression, guilt, etc.)

What are your wisest choices regarding sexual involvement?
"Either marriage, with complete faithfulness to your partner, or else total abstinence."
                                                C. S. Lewis, Mere Christianity

MARRIAGE & DIVORCE

8

1. What is marriage?

2. Do you plan to marry some day? If so, why?

3. How do you know if you are ready for marriage?

4. Why are so many people living together without being married?

What Does The Bible Say About Marriage and Divorce?

1. **Matthew 19:4-5 (NIV)** - "Haven't you read," he replied, "that at the beginning the Creator 'made them male and female,' and said, 'For this reason a man will leave his father and mother and be united to his wife, and the two will become one flesh'?

2. **Ephesians 5:22, 25, 28 (NKJV)** - Wives, submit to your own husbands, as to the Lord. . . , Husbands, love your wives, just as Christ also loved the church and gave Himself for her, . . . So husbands ought to love their own wives as their own bodies; he who loves his wife loves himself.

3. **Matthew 5:32 (ESV)** - But I say to you that everyone who divorces his wife, except on the ground of sexual immorality, makes her commit adultery, and whoever marries a divorced woman commits adultery.

I. Biblical View of Marriage

A. Marriage is between a _____ and a _____.
   Genesis 1:27-28

   Genesis 2:21-24 - So the LORD God caused a deep sleep to fall upon the man, and while he slept took one of his ribs and closed up its place with flesh. And the rib that the LORD God had taken from the man he made into a woman and brought her to the man. Then the man said, "This at last is bone of my bones and flesh of my flesh; she shall be called Woman, because she was taken out of Man." Therefore a man shall leave his father and his mother and hold fast to his wife, and they shall become one flesh.

   Matthew 19:4-5 - He answered, "Have you not read that he who created them from the beginning made them male and female, and said, 'Therefore a man shall leave his father and his mother and hold fast to his wife, and the two shall become one flesh'?

B. Marriage involves a _____ union.
   1 Corinthians 7:2-4 - Now concerning the matters about which you wrote: "It is good for a man not to have sexual relations with a woman." But because of the temptation to sexual immorality, each man should have his own wife and each woman her own husband.

   What does Song of Solomon tell us about sex in marriage?
   1. The wedding night – chapter 4

   2. The picture of marital sex

   3. Do not stir up nor awaken or arouse love until it pleases? – 2:7; 3:5; 8:4. (Feelings, passion, sexual desire must not grow faster than the commitment that comes with marriage)

   4. *What can you do to keep from stirring up sexual desire prior to marriage?*

C. Marriage involves a _____ before God.
Matthew 19:6 - So they are no longer two but one flesh. What therefore God has joined together, let not man separate."

> *What is a covenant?*

D. God is a witness of weddings, whether invited or not. Matthew 19:6

E. Husband and wife are literally joined together by _____. Matthew 19:6

F. Marriage is a God-ordained institution for all people. It is the only social institution ordained by God before the fall of mankind. Genesis 2:24-25

Why Marry?

1. _____ plan. Generally it's not good to be single – Genesis 2:18, 24.

2. Companionship – _____ in all areas of life.

3. _____, one who corresponds to her mate, completes him.

4. Blending of 2 lives into 1 – oneness intellectually, socially, spiritually, physically.

5. _____.

6. Never merely for _____ gratification

7. Never as an _____.

II. Three Elements of Commitment

> There is only one statement about marriage that God includes four times in the Scriptures - (Genesis 2:24, Matthew 19:5, Mark 10:7-8, Ephesians 5:31). Therefore a man shall leave his father and his mother and hold fast to his wife, and they shall become one flesh.

> "Therefore shall a man _____ his father and his mother, and shall _____ unto his wife: and they shall be _____ flesh."

A. "LEAVING" – your parents

1. What it does not mean:

   a. That you totally _____ your parents - (Exodus 21:17; Mark 7:9-11; 1 Timothy 5:4-8).

   b. That you must _____ 1000's of miles away. (It is possible to live two doors down and "leave", but it is also possible to be miles away and yet not "leave").

2. What it does mean:

   a. Establish an _____ relationship with them.

   b. You are more concerned about your _____ ideas and approval.

   c. It means that you do not "____" to mom and dad every time you have a problem.

   d. You make the husband/wife relationship your _____ in human relationships.

B. "CLEAVING" – to your spouse

1. Dictionary: to adhere to, cling, to be faithful.

2. Society tells us that if it doesn't work to your satisfaction then simply get out!

3. God planned for marriage to last a _____. Mark 10:7-9 – Therefore a man shall leave his father and mother and hold fast to his wife, and the two shall become one flesh. So they are no longer two but one flesh. What therefore God has joined together, let not man separate.

4. Cleaving until "_____ do us part."

C. "WEAVING" – one flesh

1. At its most elementary level this does refer to the _____ or physical union - (Song of Solomon; 1 Corinthians 6:16
   1 Corinthians 7:1-5 - Now for the matters you wrote about: It is good for a man not to marry. But since there is so much immorality, each man should have his own wife, and each woman her own husband. The husband should fulfill his marital duty to his wife, and likewise the wife to her husband. The wife's body does not belong to her alone but also to

her husband. In the same way, the husband's body does not belong to him alone but also to his wife. Do not deprive each other except by mutual consent and for a time, so that you may devote yourselves to prayer. Then come together again so that Satan will not tempt you because of your lack of self-control.

2. It means _____ than just the marriage act! In a marriage relationship we share _____.

What are some of the things that husband and wife share?

a. _____.

b. _____.

c. _____.

d. _____ & struggles.

e. Your _____!

7 Keys to a Successful Marriage

1. _____ – Start with Christ at the center of your relationship.

2. _____ – To each other "til death do us part."

3. _____ – Honest and open.

4. Cooperation – Caring, considerate, working together as a team. As ONE flesh!

5. Conflicts – They will come so handle them with grace. Build don't tear down!

6. Consummation – Yes…the sexual element is also important.

7. _____ – Again, emphasize the spiritual growth in the relationship.

I. God's Word on DIVORCE

Are there people in your family who are divorced?

REASONS FOR THE INCREASED DIVORCE RATE

1. A Rise In _____: - Concern has shifted from the well-being of families to personal happiness and success.

2. _____ Only Lasts So Long: - Society emphasizes a romantic love that can be replaced once the excitement is gone.

3. Marriage Is _____: - With both partners working (added stress).

4. Divorce Is Socially _____: - Society encourages couples to divorce.

5. Legally A Divorce Is _____ To Obtain: - Couples can divorce simply by showing their marriage has failed (Opportunity).

"In most states the classic grounds for divorce were _____, _____, and _____. This legal foundation changed when California enacted a statute in 1969 that allowed for _____ divorce" - Kerby Anderson, Christian Ethics in Plain Language, p. 136.

A. Important Statistics - (Kerby Anderson, Christian Ethics in Plain Language, pp. 131-133, 136).

1. Every year parents of over 1 million children divorce.

2. Divorce impacts _____ socially, educationally, emotionally, economically, and spiritually.

3. "Fundamental changes in our society in the last few decades have changed divorce from rare to _____."

4. "Marriage is no longer seen as a _____; it is seen instead as a _____."

B. Several Christian Views on Divorce

What is the view of your church on divorce and remarriage?

1. Christian Agreement on Divorce

- Divorce is not _____ ideal - Malachi 2:16 - "I hate divorce, " says the LORD God of Israel . . . Matthew 19:6 - So they are no longer two, but one. Therefore what God has joined together, let man not separate." See also verse 8.

- Divorce is not permissible for _____ cause - Matthew 19:3, 9 - Some Pharisees came to him to test him. They asked, "Is it lawful for a man to divorce his wife for any and every reason?" . . . I tell you that anyone who divorces his wife, except for marital unfaithfulness, and marries another woman commits adultery."

- Divorce creates many _____.

2. Christian Disagreement on Divorce

   a. Some say there are no grounds for divorce.
   1) Divorce violates God's design for _____.

   2) Divorce breaks a _____ made before God.

   3) _____ condemned all divorce - (Mark 10:1-9; Luke 16:18).

   4) The apostle _____ condemned divorce - (1 Corinthians 7:10-13).

   5) Divorce disqualified an _____ - (1 Timothy 3:2).

   6) Divorce violates a sacred typology - Ephesians 5:32 (God takes a violation of a sacred type seriously - See Numbers 20:9-12).

   b. Others will contend that there is only _____ ground for divorce.

   1) Jesus explicitly stated _____ as grounds for divorce - (Matthew 19:9).

   2) Jesus repeated this exception in a parallel passage - (Matthew 5:32).

   3) Paul agreed with Jesus' view on divorce - (1 Corinthians 7:10, 15).

   c. Still others hold that there are many grounds for divorce.

   1) Paul approves of divorce for _____ - 1Corinthians 7:15 - But if the unbeliever leaves, let him do so. A believing man or woman is not bound in such circumstances; God has called us to live in peace.

   2) Even God "divorced" Israel for unfaithfulness - (Jeremiah 3:8; Isaiah 50:1).

3) The Bible recognizes human frailty.

4) Repentance changes the situation. There is only one unpardonable sin (Matthew 12:32), and it is not _____.

Can a pastor be divorced? Can he be divorced and remarried?

How can the church help those who are divorced?

RACIAL ISSUES

Is racism still present in society today?

How do you see racism expressed in America?

How do you see racism expressed in other nations?

In what ways do churches struggle with racism?

Why do we have racism?

What Does The Bible Say About Race?

1 Corinthians 12:13 (NLT) - Some of us are Jews, some are Gentiles, some are slaves, and some are free. But we have all been baptized into one body by one Spirit, and we all share the same Spirit.

Galatians 3:28 (ESV) - There is neither Jew nor Greek, there is neither slave nor free, there is no male and female, for you are all one in Christ Jesus.

Acts 10:34,35 (NIV) - Then Peter began to speak: 'I now realize how true it is that God does not show favoritism but accepts men from every nation who fear Him and do what is right.

Acts 17:26 (NET) - From one man he made every nation of the human race to inhabit the entire earth.

John 3:16 (NIV) - For God so loved the world that he gave his one and only Son, that whoever believes in him shall not perish but have eternal life.

RACISM: The belief that certain racial distinctions determine human _____ and equal an inherent _____ or _____ of a given people.

Have you ever felt like a victim of racism?

I. How is Racism Manifested?

A. _____ – A (usually negative) overgeneralization about a certain people group as a whole based on the unaccepted behavior of a few members of that group.

> *What are some racial stereotypes?*

B. _____ – "Prejudging" an individual in a negative way because he/she happens to be from a stereotyped group.

C. _____ – Unequal treatment of a person on the basis of his/her people group membership.

> What about _____ action? – John F. Kennedy – 1961 Established the Equal Employment Opportunity Commission (EEOC) which directed that projects funded, in whole or in part, with federal funds *"take affirmative action to ensure that applicants are employed, and employees are treated during their employment without regard to race, creed, color or national origin."* This was the first use of the term "affirmative action."

> Weak to moderate

> Strong – preferential, quotas

D. _____ – Verbal and physical abuse directed toward people. This is considered justified on the basis of their group membership.

II. What is The Basis For Racism?

A. _____ **Beliefs** - That a certain people group as a whole is intellectually or morally inferior.

B. _____ **(Ethnocentrism)** - Especially in inherited traits and culture (See I Corinthians 4:7). It is the tendency to look at the world primarily from the perspective of one's own ethnic culture.

The feeling that one's group has a mode of living, values, and patterns of adaptation that are superior to those of other groups. It is coupled with a generalized contempt for members of other groups. Ethnocentrism may manifest itself in attitudes of superiority or sometimes hostility. Violence, discrimination, proselytizing, and verbal aggressiveness are other means whereby ethnocentrism may be expressed (Encyclopedia.com)

C. _____

1) Educational

"the evolutionary view that life can evolve to 'higher' levels provides fuel for racist ideas. The Bible on the other hand, clearly shows the fallacy of racism… this misleading concept gives rise to the idea that some 'races' have developed and become more sophisticated faster than others, leading to the ultimate conclusion (often subconsciously) that certain 'races' are superior"

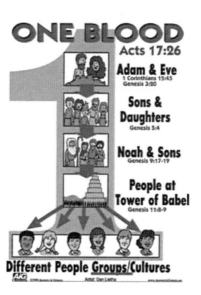

Found in answersingenesis.org

2) Voluntary

3) Biblical – Curse on _____? Or Canaan? - See Genesis 9:18-27; 10:6; Joshua 9:23. See also Acts 17:26; Galatians 3:28; Ephesians 2:14; Colossians 3:11; James 2:1-13

D. _____

1) Of unknown

2) Of what is different

What do people really fear from those who are of different skin color?

3) Of upsetting family or friends

73

E. Socialization

   1) Parental example

   2) Uncritically accepted social assumptions

Acts 17:26 (KJV) - *"And has made of one blood all nations of men for to dwell on all the face of the earth."*

III. Combating Racism with Biblical Truth

A. **Abrahamic Covenant**

answersingenesis.org

Genesis 12:1-3 - The LORD had said to Abram, "Leave your country, your people and your father's household and go to the land I will show you. I will make you into a great nation and I will bless you; I will make your name great, and you will be a blessing. will bless those who bless you, and whoever curses you I will curse; and all peoples on earth will be blessed through you. " See also Genesis 15:5-6.

Romans 4:17-18

Galatians 3:26-29 - You are all sons of God through faith in Christ Jesus, for all of you who were baptized into Christ have clothed yourselves with Christ. There is neither Jew nor Greek, slave nor free, male nor female, for you are all one in Christ Jesus. If you belong to Christ, then you are Abraham's seed, and heirs according to the promise.

B. **Mosaic Law** - Exodus 23:9 - You must not oppress foreigners. You know what it's like to be a foreigner, for you yourselves were once foreigners in the land of Egypt.

C. **Mission of Israel** - O sing unto the LORD a new song; sing unto the LORD, all the earth. Sing unto the LORD, bless His name; show forth His salvation from day to day. Declare His glory among the heathen, His wonders among all people. For the LORD is great and greatly to be praised; He is to be feared above all gods.

D. **Jesus' Example** - John 4:1-10 (The Samaritan woman at the well).

E. **Jesus' Teaching** - Luke 10:25-37 (Parable of the Good Samaritan).

Matthew 28:19 - Go therefore and make disciples of all nations, baptizing them in the name of the Father and of the Son and of the Holy Spirit

F. **The _____ breaks down divisive barriers and unifies races**

Acts 10:34-35 - So Peter opened his mouth and said: "Truly I understand that God shows no partiality, but in every nation anyone who fears him and does what is right is acceptable to him.

Acts 15:7-9 - And after there had been much debate, Peter stood up and said to them, "Brothers, you know that in the early days God made a choice among you, that by my mouth the Gentiles should hear the word of the gospel and believe. And God, who knows the heart, bore witness to them, by giving them the Holy Spirit just as he did to us, and he made no distinction between us and them, having cleansed their hearts by faith.

Acts 17:26 - And He hath made of one blood all nations of men to dwell on all the face of the earth, and hath determined the times before appointed, and the bounds of their habitation

Unity comes through the blood of Christ.

We are all one in Christ – Galatians 3:28; Colossians 3:9-15

See also Romans 1:14-16; 1 Corinthians 12:13; Ephesians 2:13-20

G. **_____ will be a multicultural celebration of Christ!!**

Revelation 5:9-10 - And they sang a new song, saying, "Worthy are you to take the scroll and to open its seals, for you were slain, and by your blood you ransomed people for God from every tribe and language and people and nation, and you have made them a kingdom and priests to our God, and they shall reign on the earth."

Revelation 7:9 - After this I looked, and behold, a great multitude that no one could number, from every nation, from all tribes and peoples and languages, standing before the throne and before the Lamb, clothed in white robes, with palm branches in their hands, and crying out with a loud voice, "Salvation belongs to our God who sits on the throne, and to the Lamb!"

H. **Racism is a _____** – James 2:8-9 - If you really fulfill the royal law according to the Scripture, "You shall love your neighbor as yourself," you are doing well. But if you show partiality, you are committing sin and are convicted by the law as transgressors.

What are some practical conclusions that Christians ought to make because of what Scripture says?

IV. Key Issues For The Church

A. Interracial Marriage

1) Marry _____ – A woman is bound to her husband as long as he lives. But if her husband dies, she is free to marry anyone she wishes, but he must belong to the Lord – 1 Corinthians 7:39.

2) What is a _____ marriage? – Do not intermarry with them. Do not give your daughters to their sons or take their daughters for your sons, for they will turn your sons away from following me to serve other gods, and the LORD's anger will burn against you and will quickly destroy you – Deuteronomy 7:3-4. See also Exodus 12:48-49. Do not be yoked together with unbelievers. For what do righteousness and wickedness have in common? Or what fellowship can light have with dark-ness? – 2 Corinthians 6:14. See also Colossians 3:9-11.

3) What are some questions to ask?
   - What are your cultural differences?
   - What do your families think about the marriage?
   - What are the consequences for your children?

4) Notice Numbers 12:1, 10a. Miriam and Aaron began to talk against Moses because of his Cushite wife, for he had married a Cushite. When the cloud lifted from above the Tent, there stood Miriam—leprous, like snow.

5) *What does the Bible say about the problems of interracial marriages?*

B. Racial _____ among believers

1) Why do believers of different races struggle to be in the same church together?

2) There are cultural differences, but they must not be practiced at the expense of unity.

76

3) Obstacles that block progress (from Tony Evans – Can We Really Get Along? – an article taken from his book <u>Let's Get To Know Each Other</u>)

  ➢ Our fear of losing our racial distinction

  ➢ Our cultural prejudice

  ➢ Our fear of the price tag of unity

  ➢ Our hesitancy to hold people accountable for racial prejudice

4) Jesus' example in John 4

5) Our priority – A new command I give you: Love one another. As I have loved you, so you must love one another. By this all men will know that you are my disciples, if you love one another" – John 13:34-35. See also Luke 10:30-37; James 2:1-13.

ALCOHOL & DRUG ABUSE

10

After you graduate from Liberty, do you plan to drink alcohol? Why or why not?

Should a Christian drink alcohol? Why or why not?

What Does The Bible Say About Alcohol and Drugs?

Proverbs 23:29-35 (NLT) - Who has anguish? Who has sorrow? Who is always fighting? Who is always complaining? Who has unnecessary bruises? Who has bloodshot eyes? It is the one who spends long hours in the taverns, trying out new drinks. Don't let the sparkle and smooth taste of wine deceive you. For in the end it bites like a poisonous serpent; it stings like a viper. You will see hallucinations, and you will say crazy things. You will stagger like a sailor tossed at sea, clinging to a swaying mast. And you will say, "They hit me, but I didn't feel it. I didn't even know it when they beat me up. When will I wake up so I can have another drink?""

I. Drug Abuse

TOBACCO : biggest killer (400,000 deaths/year)
ALCOHOL : most widely abused legal substance
PRESCRIPTION DRUGS : dangerously addictive, rising in popularity
METHAMPHETAMINE : become a drug of choice, meth labs seizures up
MARIJUANA : most widely abused illegal substance
MDMA (ECSTASY) : little research on long term effects, still popular
CRACK COCAINE : cheap, destructive drug making a comeback
HEROIN : highly addictive drug making a comeback in some areas
STEROIDS : horrible side effects, the toll they're taking on athletics
INHALANTS : abuse is on the rise among youth again

toptenstreetdrugs.org

Past Month Illicit Drug Use among Persons Aged 12 or Older: 2010

U.S. Department of Health and Human Services Substance Abuse and Mental Health Administration

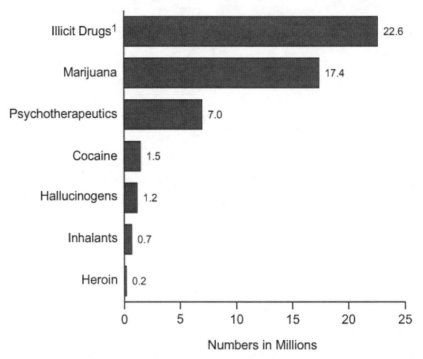

Numbers in Millions

[1] Illicit Drugs include marijuana/hashish, cocaine (including crack), heroin, hallucinogens, inhalants, or prescription-type psychotherapeutics used nonmedically.

- The overall rate of current illicit drug use among persons aged 12 or older in 2010 (8.9 percent) was similar to the rate in 2009 (8.7 percent), but it was higher than the rates in 2002 through 2008

Do you know someone who has done drugs? What kind? What effect?

II. Alcohol Abuse

National Institute on Alcohol Abuse and Alcoholism:

"The tradition of drinking has developed into a kind of culture—beliefs and customs—entrenched in every level of college students' environments. Customs handed down through generations of college drinkers reinforce students' expectation that alcohol is a necessary ingredient for social success. These beliefs and the expectations they engender exert a powerful influence over students' behavior toward alcohol.

Customs that promote college drinking also are embedded in numerous levels of students' environments. The walls of college sports arenas carry advertisements from alcohol industry sponsors. Alumni carry on the alcohol tradition, perhaps less flamboyantly than during their college years, at sports events and alumni social functions. Communities permit establishments near campus to serve or sell alcohol, and these establishments depend on the college clientele for their financial success.

Students derive their expectations of alcohol from their environment and from each other, as they face the insecurity of establishing themselves in a new social milieu. Environmental and peer influences combine to create a culture of drinking. This culture actively promotes drinking, or passively promotes it, through tolerance, or even tacit approval, of college drinking as a rite of passage."   collegedrinkingprevention.gov

"Although 40 percent of college freshmen say they binge drink -- five or more drinks on one occasion -- a new study has found than up to 20 percent of male students go far beyond the binge-drinking threshold, consuming more than 10 or 15 drinks per drinking session.

Binge drinking is usually defined as four or more drinks per occasion for females and five or more drinks for males. New research has found that a considerable number of students, particularly males, drink well beyond the 'standard' binge-drinking threshold."
June 2006 issue of *Alcoholism: Clinical & Experimental Research*.

The **alcohol statistics** below speak for themselves: alcoholabuse.com
- 33% of current drinkers had 5 or more drinks on at least one day in 2006.
- There were 21, 634 alcohol-induced deaths, excluding accidents and homicides in 2005.
- In 2005 there were 12,928 alcohol liver disease deaths.
- In 2007, there were 12,998 drunk driving fatalities.
- From 2001-2005, an average of 36 fatalities occurred per day on America's roadways as a result of crashes involving an alcohol impaired driver; 45 per day during the Christmas period ; 54 per day over the New Year's holiday.
- Alcohol kills 6 1/2 times more youth than all other illicit drugs combined.
- Three in every 10 Americans will be involved in an alcohol-related crash in their lives.
- Over 1.46 million drivers were arrested in 2006 for driving under the influence of alcohol or narcotics. This is an arrest rate of 1 for every 139 licensed drivers in the United States.
- More than 10% of Americans experience alcohol abuse or alcohol dependence at some time in their lives.

- Nearly 14 million Americans meet diagnostic criteria for alcohol use disorders.

Sources of Alcohol Statistics

1. National Center for Health Statistics
2. National Highway Traffic Safety Administration
3. Mothers Against Drunk Driving
4. National Institute on Alcohol Abuse and Alcoholism Analysis
5. Alcohol Health & Research World

Current, Binge, and Heavy Alcohol Use among Persons Aged 12 or Older, by Age: 2010 U.S. Department of Health and Human Services Substance Abuse and Mental Health Administration

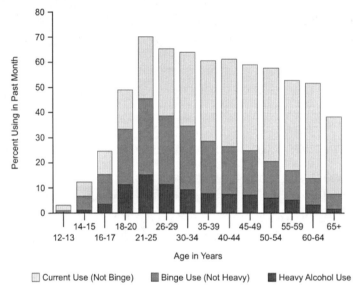

Binge Alcohol Use among Adults Aged 18 to 22, by College Enrollment: 2002-2010

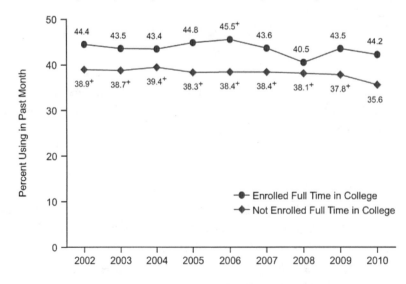

Why is drinking so important for so many college students?

College drinking problems

- About four out of five college students drink alcohol.
- About half of college students who drink, also consume alcohol through binge drinking.
  Each year, drinking affects college students, as well as college communities, and families. The consequences of drinking include:
- **Death:** 1,825 college students between the ages of 18 and 24 die each year from alcohol-related unintentional injuries.
- **Assault:** More than 690,000 students between the ages of 18 and 24 are assaulted by another student who has been drinking.
- **Sexual Abuse:** More than 97,000 students between the ages of 18 and 24 are victims of alcohol-related sexual assault or date rape.
- **Injury:** 599,000 students between the ages of 18 and 24 receive unintentional injuries while under the influence of alcohol.
- **Academic Problems:** About 25 percent of college students report academic consequences of their drinking including missing class, falling behind, doing poorly on exams or papers, and receiving lower grades overall.
- **Health Problems/Suicide Attempts:** More than 150,000 students develop an alcohol-related health problem and between 1.2 and 1.5 percent of students indicate that they tried to commit suicide within the past year due to drinking or drug use.
- **Drunk Driving:** 2.8 million students between the ages of 18 and 24 reported driving under the influence of alcohol.

III. Effects of Alcohol - *science.howstuffworks.com*

.02-.03% - No loss of coordination. May experience slight "buzz" and loss of shyness.

.04-.06% May experience a "buzz", feeling of well-being, relaxation, lowered inhibitions, sensation of warmth, minor impairment of reasoning and memory, lowering of caution.

.07-.09% Legally intoxicated in most states. May experience a slight impairment of balance, speech, vision, reaction time, and hearing. Also experience reduced judgment and self-control. Definite impairment of muscle coordination and driving skills. Increased risk of nausea and slurred speech.

.10% Clear deterioration of reaction time and control. Legal Intoxication. [.10% is at or beyond the legal limit in all 50 states.]

.10-.12% May experience a buzz, significant impairment of motor coordination, loss of good judgment, slurred speech, impaired balance, vision, reaction time and hearing.

.13-.15% The buzz is reduced. Replaced with anxiety and restlessness. Gross motor impairment, lack of physical control, blurred vision, major loss of balance. Risk of blackouts and accidents.

.16-.24% Anxiety and restlessness predominates. Nausea may appear "Sloppy drunk."

.25-.29% May experience anxiety and restlessness, total mental confusion. Need assistance in walking. Nausea and vomiting.

.30-.39% May experience loss of consciousness.

.4% and up May experience onset of coma. Death due to respiratory arrest.

IV. Alcohol and the Christian

1. You cannot compare drinking alcohol today to drinking alcohol in _____ times. (1 part wine to 3 parts water) Therefore it cannot be used for justification of drinking.

2. _____ is wrong/sin – Galatians 5:19-21 - Now the works of the flesh are evident: sexual immorality, impurity, sensuality, idolatry, sorcery, enmity, strife, jealousy, fits of anger, rivalries, dissensions, divisions, envy, drunkenness, orgies, and things like these. I warn you, as I warned you before, that those who do such things will not inherit the kingdom of God. See also Deuteronomy 21:18-21; 1 Corinthians 6:9-11

3. Clear-mindedness is the standard – 1 Peter 5:8 - Be sober-minded; be watchful. Your adversary the devil prowls around like a roaring lion, seeking someone to devour. See also Luke 22:34-36; 1 Peter 1:13

4. There is no clear command for _____ _____ for believers. (i.e.; medicinal - Proverbs 31:6 - Give strong drink to the one who is perishing, and wine to those in bitter distress.1 Timothy 5:23 - No longer drink only water, but use a little wine for the sake of your stomach and your frequent ailments.

5. General warnings in Scripture are against drinking; they are not neutral - Proverbs 20:1 - Wine is a mocker, strong drink a brawler, and whoever is led astray by it is not wise. See also Proverbs 23:30-33.

6. Principle of brotherly love - Causing your brother to _____ - Romans 14:21 - It is good not to eat meat or drink wine or do anything that causes your brother to stumble.

7. In the U.S. drinking is a sin (also a crime) for anyone under the age of _____ - 1 Peter 2:13-15 - Be subject for the Lord's sake to every human institution, whether it be to the emperor as supreme, or to governors as sent by him to punish those who do evil and to praise those who do good. For this is the will of God, that by doing good you should put to silence the ignorance of foolish people.

8. Freedom can become a _____ if it breaks institutional rules (i.e., parents' rules, Liberty Way) - 1 Peter 2:13-15.

9. Those dedicated to God's service should abstain - Numbers 6:2-3; Leviticus 10:9; Ezekiel 44:21; Judges 13:4-5; Proverbs 31:4-5; Luke 1:15. It is interesting to remember - believers are a priesthood 1 Peter 2:9.

10. Everything a believer does should be done to the "_____ of God" - 1 Corinthians 10:31 - So, whether you eat or drink, or whatever you do, do all to the glory of God.

V. Why Christians Need Not Drink Alcohol - Norman Geisler

- People today have plenty of wholesome, _____ beverages.

- We live in an alcoholic culture.

- _____ is the safer policy.

- Abstinence is a more consistent policy.

> (See Norman Geisler's article (A Christian Perspective on Wine-Drinking" - http://therev.home.mindspring.com/studies/wine.pdf)

And do not get drunk with wine, for that is debauchery, but be filled with the Spirit – **Ephesians 5:18 (ESV)**

What the Bible Says About Drinking Wine or Other Strong Drink

I. Uses of Wine in the Bible
- A. Wine was made from grapes (Gen. 40:11; 49:11) and pomegranates (Song 8:2).
- B. Wines were used at meals (Gen. 27:25; Matt. 26:27-29; Mark 14:23).
- C. Jesus made wine at the marriage feast in Cana (John 2).
- D. Wine was used for medicinal purposes (Prov. 31:6-7; I Tim 5:23).
- E. Melchizedek gave wine to Abraham (Gen. 14:18).
- F. Wine was offered with sacrifices (Ex. 29:40; Lev. 23:13; Num. 15:5, 10; 28:7, 14).
- G. Cheap wine (like vinegar) was given to Jesus at the crucifixion (Matt. 27:48; Mark 15:23; Luke 23:36; John 19:29).
- H. Wine was used in communion in the early church (I Cor. 11:21-22).

I. Wine was used figuratively of:
   1. Divine judgments (Psa. 60:3; 75:8; Jer. 51:7)
   2. Of the joy of wisdom (Prov. 9:2,5)
   3. Of the joys of spiritual matters (Isa. 25:6; 55:1; Joel 2:19)
   4. Of abominations (Rev. 14:8; 16:19)
II. Warnings Against Drunkenness
   A. Overseers must not be given to drunkenness (I Tim. 3:3; Titus 1:7).
   B. Deacons are not to be indulging in much wine (I Tim. 3:8).
   C. Believers are not to be controlled by wine (Eph. 5:18).
   D. Older women are not to be addicted to much wine (Titus 2:3).
III. Sobriety (Clear-mindedness)
   A. Commanded (I Pet. 1:13; I Pet. 5:8)
   B. The Gospel is designed to teach sobriety (Titus 2:12).
   C. Sobriety is linked to watchfulness (I Thess. 5:6).
   D. Sobriety is necessary to be able to pray (I Pet. 4:7).
   E. Sobriety is required in:
      1. God's servants (I Tim. 3:2-3; Titus 1:8; 2:12)
      2. Wives of servants of God (I Tim. 3:11)
      3. Aged men (Titus 2:2)
      4. Young men (Titus 2:6)
      5. Young women (Titus 2:4)
      6. All saints (I Thess. 5:6,8)
   F. We should estimate our character and talents with sobriety. (Rom. 12:3)
   G. We should live in sobriety. (Titus 2:12)
   H. The motives of sobriety (I Pet. 4:7; 5:8)
IV. Instances of Drunkenness
   A. Noah (Gen. 9:21)
   B. Lot (Gen. 19:13)
   C. Nabal (I Sam. 25:36)
   D. Uriah (II Sam. 11:13)
   E. Elah (I King 16:9)
   F. Ben-hadad and his thirty-two confederate kings (I Kings 20:16)
   G. Ahasuerus (Est. 1:10-11)
   H. Belshazzar (Dan. 5:1-6)
   I. Priests during Isaiah's time (Isa. 28:7)
   J. Church of Corinth (I Cor. 11:21-22)
   K. Falsely Accused
      1. Hannah (I Sam. 1:12-16)
      2. Jesus (Matt. 11:19)
      3. The Apostles (Acts 2:13-15)
V. General Warnings About Drinking
   A. Proverbs 20:1
   B. Proverbs 21:17
   C. Proverbs 23:20
   D. Proverbs 23:30-31
   E. Romans 14:19-23
   F. I Corinthians 10:31
VI. Abstinence Demanded
   A. Nazarites (Num. 6:2-3); (Samson, Samuel, John the Baptist)
   B. Priests while on duty (Lev. 10:9; Ezek. 44:21) See Lev. 10:1-8
   C. Samson's mother (Judges 13:4-5)
   D. Rulers (Prov. 31:4-5)
   E. John the Baptist (Luke 1:15)
VII. Abstinence Practiced
   A. Daniel (Dan. 1:5,8,16; 10:3)
   B. Courtiers of Ahasuerus (Est. 1:10-11)
   C. Timothy (I Tim. 5:23)
   D. John the Baptist (Luke 1:1

POVERTY

Describe a poor person.

Why are some people poor?

Is it wrong to be wealthy?

What Does The Bible Say About The Poor?

Proverbs 14:20, 21, 31 (NIV) - The poor are shunned even by their neighbors, but the rich have many friends. He who despises his neighbor sins, but blessed is he who is kind to the needy. He who oppresses the poor shows contempt for their Maker, but whoever is kind to the needy honors God.

Matthew 25:31-46 (NIV) – 35 - For I was hungry and you gave me something to eat, I was thirsty and you gave me something to drink, I was a stranger and you invited me in

Galatians 2:10 (NLT) They requested only that we remember the poor, the very thing I also was eager to do.

I.   Facts About Poverty

✓ 72% of Americans consider poverty to be a serious social problem
✓ 13% of Americans live in poverty

www.barna.org

✓ About 25,000 people die of hunger every day across the world

✓ If 22 developed countries each gave 0.7% of their income to fight hunger and disease, poverty could be wiped out

www.poverty.com

11 Facts about Global Poverty

1. Nearly half the world – over three billion people – live on less than $2.50 a day.
2. According to UNICEF, 26,500-30,000 children die each day due to poverty – that's 18 children dying every minute, a child every three seconds.
3. About 1.1 billion people in developing countries have inadequate access to water, and 2.6 billion lack basic sanitation.
4. For the 1.9 billion children from the developing world: 640 million are without adequate shelter, 400 million do not have access to safe water, 270 million do not have access to health services.
5. About 2.2 million children die each year because they are not immunized.
6. About 1.6 billion people – a quarter of humanity – live without electricity.
7. Over nine million people, of which five million are children, die worldwide each year because of hunger and malnutrition.
8. Over 11 million children die each year from preventable causes like malaria, diarrhea and pneumonia.
9. About 20% of the population in the developed nations consume 86% of the world's goods.
10. The poorest 40% of the world's population accounts for 5% of the global income. The richest 20% accounts for 75% of world income.
11. Around 27-28% of all children in developing countries are estimated to be underweight or stunted.

Sources: <u>Global Issues</u> <u>Poverty.com</u>

Measures of Poverty

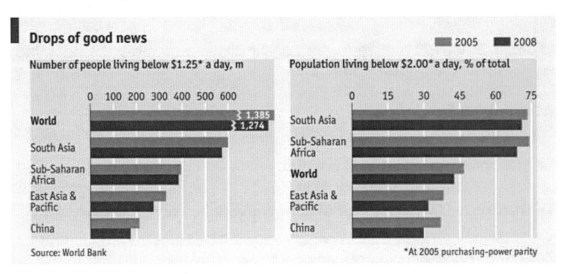

Drops of good news   ■ 2005 ■ 2008

Number of people living below $1.25* a day, m

Population living below $2.00* a day, % of total

Source: World Bank

*At 2005 purchasing-power parity

Number of hungry people in the world

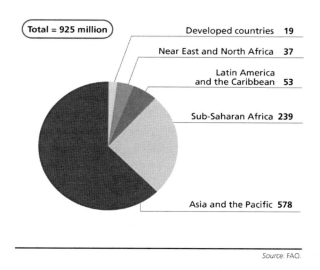

Total = 925 million

Developed countries	19
Near East and North Africa	37
Latin America and the Caribbean	53
Sub-Saharan Africa	239
Asia and the Pacific	578

Source: FAO.

United Nations Environment Programme (UNEP) – Global Environment Outlook 2000

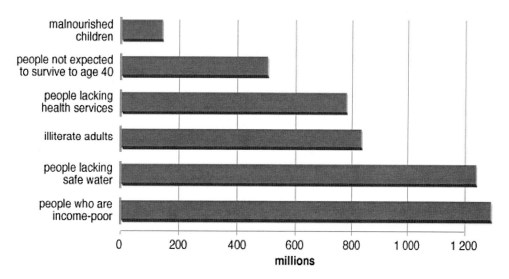

Facts about children and poverty - www.globalissues.org

Over 25,000 people (mostly children) die every day around the world. That is equivalent to:

- 1 child dying every 3.5 seconds
- 17-18 children dying every minute
- A 2004 Asian Tsunami occurring almost every 1.5 weeks
- An Iraq-scale death toll every 16–38 days
- Over 9 million children dying every year
- Some 70 million children dying between 2000 and 2007

II. Causes of Poverty

The underlying causes of poverty are a controversial, politicized issue. Many different factors have been cited to explain why poverty occurs. No single explanation has gained universal acceptance. The factors that have been alleged to cause poverty include: state discrimination and corruption, abuse of public power, lack of social integration, competition instead of co-operation, crime, natural factors such as climate or environment, historical factors, for example imperialism and colonialism, overpopulation, war, including civil war, genocide, etc.   www.connect-world.net

Kerby Anderson – causes of poverty from the Bible

1. _____ and fraud.

2. _____, persecution, or judgment.

3. _____, neglect, or gluttony.

4. Culture of _____, poverty breeds poverty.

www.probe.org (Wealth and Poverty)

III. Biblical Observations on Poverty

1. Poverty is _____.

    There will always be poor people in the land. Therefore I command you to be openhanded toward your brothers and toward the poor and needy in your land – Deuteronomy 15:11. See also Matthew 26:11; Mark 14:7; John 12:8.

2. Poverty may be a consequence of _____ personal choices (but not always).

    Lazy hands make a man poor, but diligent hands bring wealth – Proverbs 10:4.
    Lazy people sleep soundly, but idleness leaves them hungry – Proverbs 19:15.

3. Poverty may be a consequence of sinful choices made by _____ (but not always).

    James 5:1-4

4. Poverty is not _____.

_____ was poor – You know the generous grace of our Lord Jesus Christ. Though he was rich, yet for your sakes he became poor, so that by his poverty he could make you rich – 2 Corinthians 8:9. See also Matthew 8:20.

5. God may have a _____ for the poor.

Listen to me, dear brothers and sisters. Hasn't God chosen the poor in this world to be rich in faith? Aren't they the ones who will inherit the Kingdom he promised to those who love him? – James 2:5.

IV. Biblical Reasons Why Christians Should Minister to the Poor

1. _____ expects it - Deuteronomy 15:11.

    OT - Leviticus 19:9-10 - When you reap the harvest of your land, you shall not reap your field right up to its edge, neither shall you gather the gleanings after your harvest. And you shall not strip your vineyard bare, neither shall you gather the fallen grapes of your vineyard. You shall leave them for the poor and for the sojourner: I am the LORD your God. Deuteronomy 24:19-22 - gleaning laws - tithe - Leviticus 27:30

    God required it of the king of Israel. Psalm 72:1-4, 12-14 - Give the king your justice, O God, and your righteousness to the royal son! May he judge your people with righteousness, and your poor with justice! Let the mountains bear prosperity for the people, and the hills, in righteousness! May he defend the cause of the poor of the people, give deliverance to the children of the needy, and crush the oppressor! . . . For he delivers the needy when he calls, the poor and him who has no helper. He has pity on the weak and the needy, and saves the lives of the needy. From oppression and violence he redeems their life, and precious is their blood in his sight.

    NT - the church – If someone has enough money to live well and sees a brother or sister in need but shows no compassion— how can God's love be in that person? – 1 John 3:17. See also 1 Corinthians 16; Acts 11:29; 4:34; 2 Corinthians 8:4.

2. Paul's example – All they asked was that we should continue to remember the poor, the very thing I was eager to do – Galatians 2:10.

3. The principle of _____ and _____ - Galatians 6:7-10; Matthew 5:7.

4. God will _____ those who give.

> He who is kind to the poor lends to the LORD, and he will reward him for what he has done – Proverbs 19:17.

> See also Proverbs 22:9, 28:27.

5. When Christians give to the poor they are giving to God - Matthew 25:31-46.

6. Giving to the poor brings _____ to the Christian – Romans 15:26 - For Macedonia and Achaia have been pleased to make some contribution for the poor among the saints at Jerusalem.

V.   The Christian Attitude toward the Poor

1. Consider others better than ourselves.

> Do nothing out of selfish ambition or vain conceit, but in humility consider others better than yourselves – Philippians 2:3.

> See also 1 Corinthians 10:24.

2. We are not to be a _____ of persons - James 2:1-9.

3. We are to _____ our neighbor as ourselves.

> Love your neighbor as yourself – Matthew 22:39b.

4. The Golden Rule.

> So in everything, do to others what you would have them do to you, for this sums up the Law and the Prophets – Matthew 7:12. See also Luke 6:31.

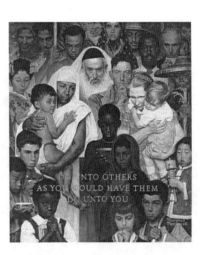

5. When you see a need, _____ it if you can.

> Anyone, then, who knows the good he ought to do and doesn't do it, sins – James 4:17. See also Luke 10 25-37.

What is the responsibility of the government and what is the responsibility of the church in helping the poor?

VI. Ten Principles To Govern Giving Assistance to the Poor Through an Organization

1. _____ – Does the program demand accountability from the people it serves?

2. _____ – Does the program stress the building of character? "Give a man a fish and feed him for a day. Teach him how to fish and feed him for a lifetime" - 2 Thessalonians 3:10; Proverbs 6:6.

3. _____ – Do the providers use judgment to give help on an individual basis?

4. _____ – Does the program require work of those who can work?

5. _____ – Does the program teach recipients how to free themselves from their dependent status?

6. _____ – Does the program foster true self-esteem by leading them to their Creator and His principles?

7. Success rate – Does the program have a success rate that can be quantified?

8. Assessment – Does the program conduct periodic assessment to determine its effectiveness?

9. _____ – How much money donated goes directly to the poor?

10. _____ – Are volunteers utilized to keep cost down and to provide a meaningful ministry for people.

Programs that help the poor are intended to be a "safety net" not a "hammock".

Galatians 2:10 - . . . they asked us to remember the poor, the very thing I was eager to do.

VII. Ten Activities to Make a Difference

1. Volunteer at a soup kitchen.

2. Open a _____ _____ and clothing center in the church.

3. _____ students and adults.

4. Provide basic job training.

5. Provide _____ care services for single parents or others who are in real need.

6. Be a _____ to children from broken homes.

7. Help with Habitat for Humanity.

8. Work with urban shelters for the _____.

9. Clean up parks and recreational facilities to provide good activities for kids and families.

10. Become informed about the specific needs of your community.

Conclusion:

Yes, we feed their bodies, but more importantly we must feed them spiritually. Not just bread made by hand but the Bread of Life (Jesus)

Isaiah 61:1 - The Spirit of the Lord GOD is upon me, because the LORD has anointed me to bring good news to the poor; he has sent me to bind up the brokenhearted, to proclaim liberty to the captives, and the opening of the prison to those who are bound.

Matthew 11:5 - the blind receive their sight and the lame walk, lepers are cleansed and the deaf hear, and the dead are raised up, and the poor have good news preached to them.

WORK ETHIC

What do you plan to do for your life work? Why?

What's Your Work Ethic

What makes a person successful in his/her work?

What Does The Bible Say About Work Ethic?

Colossians 3:22-24 (NET) – Slaves, obey your earthly masters in every respect, not only when they are watching – like those who are strictly people-pleasers – but with a sincere heart, fearing the Lord. Whatever you are doing, work at it with enthusiasm, as to the Lord and not for people, because you know that you will receive your inheritance from the Lord as the reward. Serve the Lord Christ.

Colossians 4: 1 (NET) – Masters, treat your slaves with justice and fairness, because you know that you also have a master in heaven.

2 Thessalonians 3:10-12 (NLT) – Even while we were with you, we gave you this rule: "Whoever does not work should not eat." (11) Yet we hear that some of you are living idle lives, refusing to work and wasting time meddling in other people's business. (12) In the name of the Lord Jesus Christ, we appeal to such people--no, we command them: Settle down and get to work. Earn your own living.

Biblical Ethics for Work/Business

Christian Worldview (influence) – Matthew 5:13-16 - "You are the salt of the earth, but if salt has lost its taste, how shall its saltiness be restored? It is no longer good for anything except to be thrown out and trampled under people's feet. You are the light of the world. A city set on a hill cannot be hidden. Nor do people light a lamp and put it under a basket, but on a stand, and it gives light to all in the house. In the same way, let your light shine before others, so that they may see your good works and give glory to your Father who is in heaven.

➢ Salt-Spiritual influence

➢ Light-_____

➢ What is important in work and business?

_____ you do.

_____ you do it.

_____ you do it.

❖ Definition - The applying of _____ principles or rules of conduct in business.

I. Principles Related to Business Ethics

A. A Secular View of Business Ethics

1. The ultimate purpose of work is to fulfill your self.

2. Success in _____ means success in _____.

3. Success is based on financial _____, professional recognition or _____.

4. You have to do _____ __ _____ to get the job done.

B. A Biblical View of Business Ethics

1. God is the ultimate owner of all of the world's resources - The land shall not be sold in perpetuity, for the land is mine. For you are strangers and sojourners with me. – Leviticus 25:23

2. People are responsible to care for and properly use the resources of this world – And God blessed them. And God said to them, "Be fruitful and multiply and fill the earth and subdue it, and have dominion over the fish of the sea and over the birds of the heavens and over every living thing that moves on the earth." – Genesis 1:28

3. Through work we can _____ and _____ people – Matthew 22:37-40.

4. Through work we can meet our own _____ and those of our family.

If anyone does not provide for his relatives, and especially for his immediate family, he has denied the faith and is worse than an unbeliever – 1 Timothy 5:8.
See also 2 Thessalonians 3:6-12

5. Through work we can earn money to _____ to others.

He who has been stealing must steal no longer, but must work, doing something useful with his own hands, that he may have something to share with those in need – Ephesians 4:28. See also Leviticus 19:10.

6. Through work we can bring _____ to God.

So whether you eat or drink or whatever you do, do it all for the glory of God – 1 Corinthians 10:31.

How do the issues of poverty and work ethic fit together in a biblical ethic?

Ray Cotton – Business & Ethics
Just weight – Deuteronomy 25:13-16 Total honesty – Ephesians 4:25 Being a servant – Matthew 20:28 Personal responsibility – Romans 12:2 Reasonable profit – Luke 6:31   http://www.probe.org/

C. A Biblical View of Work/Money!

1. We are _____ to work.

Make it your goal to live a quiet life, minding your own business and working with your hands, just as we instructed you before – 1 Thessalonians 4:11. See also Genesis 1:28; Exodus 20:9.

2. We are not to love the world.

Do not love this world nor the things it offers you, for when you love the world, you do not have the love of the Father in you – 1 John 2:15.

3. We must not be a _____ to money.

No one can serve two masters. Either he will hate the one and love the other, or he will be devoted to the one and despise the other. You cannot serve both God and Money – Matthew 6:24.

4. Money is not the most important _____.

But seek first his kingdom and his righteousness, and all these things will be given to you as well – Matthew 6:33. See also Matthew 22:37-40.

II. In Relation to My Work Ethic, a Biblical Worldview Will Affect:

1. How I view work – As a _____ not a _____.

   Six days you shall labor and do all your work – Exodus 20:9. See also Genesis 1:28; 1 Thessalonians 4:11; Proverbs 6:6-8.

2. How I view my employees – With _____ and _____.
   Masters, be just and fair to your slaves. Remember that you also have a Master—in heaven – Colossians 4:1. See also James 5:1-6.

3. How I view my employer – With _____ and _____.

   Slaves, obey your earthly masters in everything you do. Try to please them all the time, not just when they are watching you. Serve them sincerely because of your reverent fear of the Lord – Colossians 3:22. See also 1 Timothy 6:1; 2 Peter 2:18-19.

4. How I approach my work – As unto the Lord – Colossians 3:22-23.

5. How I do my work – with _____ and _____.

   Better to be poor and honest than to be dishonest and a fool – Proverbs 19:1. See also Proverbs 11:1; 18:9; Matthew 5:13-16.

   Do what's right, no matter what!

How do you view your job? Is the quality of your work affected by the amount of pay you receive?

III. Implementing Such a Worldview Results in God Being Glorified! Six Steps to Avoid Compromise in Business

1. Decide to do the _____ thing _____ of time – Proverbs 7:1-7.

   "Ethics takes a beating in tough times." – Graham Tucker.

2. Don't _____ evil and flirt with temptation – Proverbs 7:8-9.

3. Remember compromise is just a _____ away – Proverbs 7:10-12; Genesis 4:7.

4. Remember flattery and fantasy entices compromise – Proverbs 7:13-17.

5. Remember compromise ensnares through rationalization & _____ – Proverbs 7:18-21.

- *"Everybody* does it"
- "They _____ me one"
- "It will all come out in the wash"
- "It's the way the _____ works here"
- "Who's going to know?"

6. Remember compromise always _____ – Proverbs 7:22-27.

IV. Issues In Business Today

1. National Business Ethics

- Respect for employees and employers
- Sexual harassment
- Environmental issues
- Insider trading
- The rights of individual conscience

2. International Business Ethics

- Child labor
- Unfair wages
- Bribery
- Worker safety

V. CSER – and a Biblical Work Ethic – Applicable to ALL CSERs

1. Be _____ in your work (attitude).

2. Be on _____.

3. Be _____.

4. Be _____.

5. Be a good _____ (it reflects on):

  ❖ Christ
  ❖ Liberty
  ❖ Your Personal Character

CONFLICT RESOLUTION

Do you enjoy conflict?

What are some ways that we fail to handle conflict properly?

What Does The Bible Say About Conflict Resolution?

Romans 12:18 (NIV) - If it is possible, as far as it depends on you, live at peace with everyone.

Matthew 22:37-39 (NIV) - Jesus replied: 'Love the Lord your God with all your heart and with all your soul and with all your mind. This is the first and greatest commandment. And the second is like it: 'Love your neighbor as yourself.'

Matthew 7:12 (NIV) – So in everything, do to others what you would have them do to you, for this sums up the Law and the Prophets.

Life is 10% what happens to you and 90% how you respond!

-Chuck Swindoll

Right responses to conflict

1. _____ building

2. Selflessness

3. Reconciliation

Wrong responses to conflict

1. _____

2. _____/_____

3. Stress

4. Frustration

I. Biblical Principles

A. Love _____.

Jesus replied, You must love the Lord your God with all your heart, all your soul, and all your mind. This is the first and greatest commandment – Matthew 22:37-38. See also 1 Corinthians 10:31.

B. Love _____.

And the second is like it: 'Love your neighbor as yourself – Matthew 22:39. See also 1 Corinthians 13:4-8.

   a. cover in love

   Proverbs 10:12 - Hatred stirs up strife, but love covers all offenses.

   Proverbs 19:11 - Good sense makes one slow to anger, and it is his glory to overlook an offense.

   1 Peter 4:8 - Above all, keep loving one another earnestly, since love covers a multitude of sins.

   b. look into your own heart

   Matthew 7:5 - You hypocrite, first take the log out of your own eye, and then you will see clearly to take the speck out of your brother's eye.

   Galatians 6:1 - Brothers, if anyone is caught in any transgression, you who are spiritual should restore him in a spirit of gentleness. Keep watch on yourself, lest you too be tempted.

   c. be careful of your _____

   Proverbs 15:1 - A soft answer turns away wrath, but a harsh word stirs up anger.

   Proverbs 16:21 - The wise of heart is called discerning, and sweetness of speech increases persuasiveness.

C. Keep your _____ even when it hurts.

   who keeps his oath even when it hurts – Psalm 15:4b.

D. Respect _____ - respect the position even when the personality leaves much to be desired.

102

Obey your leaders and submit to their authority. They keep watch over you as men who must give an account. Obey them so that their work will be a joy, not a burden, for that would be of no advantage to you – Hebrews 13:17.

E. Apply the Golden Rule.

So in everything, do to others what you would have them do to you, for this sums up the Law and the Prophets. – Matthew 7:12.

II. Four Reactions to Conflict

1. "_____ WAY" - I assert my will until you give in. My way is the only way. I'm always right and must always win.

   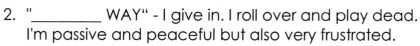

   - "It's my way or the Highway!"

   - This person _____ and refuses to listen.

2. "_____ WAY" - I give in. I roll over and play dead. I'm passive and peaceful but also very frustrated.

   - This is the opposite of the first reaction.

   - This person is usually unhappy with himself or herself and in the relationship.

   - _____ could eventually ruin this person.

3. "_____ WAY" - I withdraw. I _____ conflict at all costs. I ignore the problem. Nothing is ever resolved.

   - This person pretends the problem doesn't exist. A sense of self-denial and rationalization is their response.

   - Anthills can literally become mountains. By the time they are "forced" to respond it is too late.

4. "_____ WAY" - I care about our relationship and your needs too. So we endeavor to work out mutual goals.

   - This person is willing to listen and hopes to understand the problem and the person.

   - Confrontation motivated out of _____ & _____.

III. Assumptions on Conflict

A. You have 50% responsibility for causing and resolving the conflict.

B. Most conflicts can be resolved and many prevented using the right approach.

C. You can't change _____. You can change your own _____.

IV. Learning To Handle Conflict

A. Do everything possible not to be the _____ of conflict

If it is possible, as far as it depends on you, live at peace with everyone – Romans 12:18.

Let us therefore make every effort to do what leads to peace and to mutual edification – Romans 14:19.

Make every effort to live in peace with all men and to be holy; without holiness no one will see the Lord – Hebrews 12:14.

B. Do _____ when it is in your power to do so

Do not withhold good from those who deserve it, when it is in your power to act. Do not say to your neighbor, "Come back later; I'll give it tomorrow"—when you now have it with you – Proverbs 3:27-28.

C. Help those who _____ conflict

Brothers, if someone is caught in a sin, you who are spiritual should restore him gently. But watch yourself, or you also may be tempted – Galatians 6:1.

D. Deal with conflict _____ when it does come

Not every issue has to become a conflict

There is a biblical approach to handling the conflict.

Matthew 18:15-17 - "If your brother sins against you, go and tell him his fault, between you and him alone. If he listens to you, you have gained your brother. But if he does not listen, take one or two others along with you, that every charge may be established by the evidence of two or three witnesses. If he refuses to listen to them, tell it to the church. And if he refuses to listen even to the church, let him be to you as a Gentile and a tax collector.

How will this look in practice? What will it mean for those who are Christians? What will it not mean?

V. Steps in Conflict Resolution

    1. Define the Problem & Listen

    2. Show Respect

    3. Find Solutions

    4. Reach Agreement

    5. Follow-Through

      1. _____ to discover & define the problem.

- Do not _____ while the person is talking.

- Ask _____ to understand - Clarify!

- Restate, paraphrase, summarize facts & feelings.

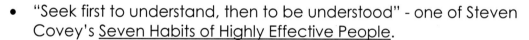

- Think of the other person's perspective.

- "Seek first to understand, then to be understood" - one of Steven Covey's <u>Seven Habits of Highly Effective People</u>.

    2. Show _____ to all participants

- The point is not who "started it" but how can we "resolve it."

- Use open body language.

- Make ____ contact.

- Face the speaker.

- Show understanding nonverbally - Watch your body language!

- Consider all differences - age, culture, background.

3. Find a _____

- Seek alternative solutions.

- Weigh pros and cons.

- Try to find _____ ground.

- Look for common goals, interest, or purpose.

- Seek mutual benefits

4. Reach _____

5. Follow Through

- Make sure that <u>you</u> follow the agreement set

PEACEFUL – conflict resolution

R – Respect the right to disagree.
E – Express your real concerns.
S – Share common goals & interests.
O – Open yourself to different points of view.
L – Listen carefully to all proposals.
U – Understand the major issue involved.
T – Think about probable consequences.
I – Imagine several possible alternative solutions.
O – Offer some reasonable compromises.
N – Negotiate mutually fair cooperative agreements.

By Robert E Valet

MORAL ISSUES RESOURCE LIST

Anderson, Kerby. *Christian Ethics in Plain Language*. Nashville: Thomas Nelson, 2005.

Beals, Art. *Beyond Hunger: A Biblical Mandate for Social Responsibility*. Portland, Oregon, Multnomah Press, 1985.

Bonevac, Daniel. *Today's Moral Issues: Classic and Contemporary Perspectives*. New York, New York: McGraw-Hill Companies, 2006.

Boss, Judith A. *Analyzing Moral Issues*. 2nd ed. Boston: McGraw-Hill Companies, 2002.

Boss, Judith A. *Ethics for Life: A Text with Readings*. Boston, McGraw-Hill Companies, 2004.

Clark, David K., and Robert V. Rakestraw. *Readings in Christian Ethics: Issues and Applications*. Vol. 2. Grand Rapids: Baker Books, 2000.

Clark, David K., and Robert V. Rakestraw. *Readings in Christian Ethics: Theory and Method*. Vol. 1. Grand Rapids: Baker Books, 2000.

Colson, Charles., and Nancy Pearcey. *How Shall We Then Live*. Wheaton: Tyndale House Publishers, 1999.

Evan, Tony. *Let's Get To Know Each Other: What White and Black Christians Need to Know About Each Other*. Nashville: Thomas Nelson Publishers, 1995.

Feinberg, John S. and Paul D. *Ethics for a Brave New World*. Wheaton, Illinois: Crossway Books, 2010.

Geisler, Norman L. *Christian Ethics: Contemporary Issues and Options*. Grand Rapids: Baker Books, 2010.

Gibbs, David. *Fighting for Dear Life: The Untold Story of Terri Schiavo and What It Means for All of Us*. Minneapolis, Minnesota: Bethany House, 2006.

Gordon, Wayne L. *Real Hope in Chicago*. Grand Rapids, Michigan: Zondervan Publishing House, 1995.

Green, Joel B., gen. ed. *Dictionary of Scripture and Ethics*. Grand Rapids, Michigan: Baker Academic, 2011.

Grudem, Wayne. *Business for the Glory of God: The Bible's Teaching on the Moral Goodness of Business*. Wheaton, Illinois: Crossway, 2003.

_____. *Countering the Claims of Evangelical Feminism: Biblical Responses to the Key Questions*. Colorado Springs, Colorado: Multnomah Publishers, 2006.

_____. *Politics According to the Bible: A Comprehensive Resource for Understanding Modern Political Issues in Light of Scripture*. Grand Rapids, Michigan: Zondervan, 2010.

Harris, Joshua. *I Kissed Dating Goodbye*. Sisters, Oregon: Multnomah Books, 1997.

Heimbach, Daniel R. *True Sexual Morality: Recovering Biblical Standards for a Culture in Crisis*. Wheaton, Illinois: Crossway Books, 2004.

Hogsett, Jim A. *A Worker Need Not Be Ashamed: How to Live the Christian Life in the Workplace*. 1st Books, 2004.

Hollinger, Dennis. *Choosing the Good: Christian Ethics in a Complex World*. Grand Rapids, Michigan: Baker Academic, 2002.

_____. *The Meaning of Sex: Christian Ethics and the Moral Life*. Grand Rapids, Michigan: Baker Academic, 2009.

Humphrey, Derek. *Dying with Dignity: Understanding Euthanasia*. New York: Carol Publishing Group, 1992.

Kilner John F. *Why The Church Needs Bioethics: A Guide to Wise Engagement with Life's Challenges*. Grand Rapids, Michigan: Zondervan, 2011.

Kostenberger, Andreas J. *God, Marriage, and Family: Rebuilding the Biblical Foundation*. Wheaton, Illinois: Crossway Books, 2004.

Lapin, Daniel. *America's Real War*. Sisters, Oregon: Multnomah Publishers, 1999.

Levine, Carol. *Taking Sides: Clashing Views on Bioethical Issues*. Dubuque, Iowa: McGraw-Hill Company, 2008.

Murray, John. *Principles of Conduct: Aspects of Biblical Ethics*. Grand Rapids, Michigan: William B. Eerdmans Publishing Company, 1957.

Pearcey, Nancy. *Total Truth: Liberating Christianity from Its Cultural Captivity*. Wheaton, Illinois: Crossway Books, 2004.

Piper, John. *Bloodlines: Race, Cross, and the Christian*. Wheaton, Illinois: Crossway, 2011.

Piper, John and Wayne Grudem, ed. *Recovering Biblical Manhood and Womanhood: A Response to Evangelical Feminism*. Wheaton, Illinois: Crossway Books, 1991, 2006.

Rae, Scott B. *Moral Choices: An Introduction to Ethics*. Grand Rapids, Michigan: Zondervan, 2009.

Satris, Stephen. *Taking Sides: Clashing Views on Moral Issues*. Dubuque, Iowa: McGraw-Hill Company, 2008.

Shapiro, Ben. *Brainwashed: How Universities Indoctrinate America's Youth*. Nashville: WND Books, 2004.

Swindoll, Charles R. *Sanctity of Life The Inescapable Issue*. Dallas: Word Publishing, 1990.

Talley, Jim A. and Bobbie Reed. *Too Close Too Soon: Avoiding the Heartache of Premature Intimacy*. Nashville: Thomas Nelson Publishers, 2002.

VanDrunen, David. *Bioethics and the Christian Life: A Guide to Making Difficult Decisions*. Wheaton, Illinois: Crossway, 2009.

Wilkens, Steve. *Beyond Bumper Sticker Ethics*. Downers Grove: Intervarsity Press, 1995.

Williams, Jarvis J. *One New Man: The Cross and Racial Reconciliation in Pauline Theology*. Nashville, Tennesse: B&H Academic, 2010.